ACOUSTIC GUITAR MAGAZINE'S
private lessons

ACOUSTIC GUITAR ACCOMPANIMENT BASICS

STRING LETTER PUBLISHING

Publisher: David A. Lusterman
Editorial Director: Jeffrey Pepper Rodgers
Editor: Scott Nygaard
Managing Editor: Simone Solondz
Music Editor: Andrew DuBrock
Designer: Gary Cribb
Production Coordinator: Christi Payne

Music Engraving: Andrew DuBrock
Cover photo: Alan Messer, courtesy Bourgeois Guitars
Photographs: Rory Earnshaw (Dix Bruce), Willie Floyd (Dylan Schorer), Bill Gribble (John Gribble), David Johnston (Elizabeth Papapetrou), Patrick O'Connor (David Hamburger)

© 1999 by String Letter Publishing, Inc.
David A. Lusterman, Publisher
ISBN 1-890490-11-3

Printed in the United States of America.
All rights reserved. This book was produced by String Letter Publishing, Inc.,
PO Box 767, San Anselmo, California 94979-0767.
(415) 485-6946; www.acousticguitar.com

STRING LETTER PUBLISHING

contents

- 4 **CD Track List**
- 5 **Introduction**
- 6 **Music Notation Key**
- 9 **About the Teachers**

GETTING STARTED

- 11 **Folk Song Accompaniment** HAPPY TRAUM
  - 12 *Down in the Valley*
- 18 **Country Backup, Carter Style** DIX BRUCE
  - 20 *Worried Man Blues*
  - 23 *Gold Watch and Chain*
- 25 **Accompanying Your Voice** ELIZABETH PAPAPETROU
  - 26 *Wildwood Flower*
- 29 **Speeding Up Chord Changes** JANET SMITH
  - 30 *Tom Dooley*

MOVING ON

- 32 **Tackling Barre Chords** JOHN GRIBBLE
  - 35 *Down in the Valley*
- 37 **Moving Bass Lines** HAPPY TRAUM
  - 38 *The Water Is Wide*
  - 40 *Mr. Bojangles*
- 42 **Using a Capo** DAVID HAMBURGER
- 47 **Rock Rhythm** DAVID HAMBURGER
- 53 **Chord Embellishment** DYLAN SCHORER
  - 56 *Star of the County Down*
  - 58 *June Apple*

- 60 **Basic Chord Library**

CD track list

Track Numbers	Lesson		Played by
1	**Introduction and Tune-up**		SCOTT NYGAARD
2–15	**Folk Song Accompaniment**		HAPPY TRAUM
	3	*Down in the Valley*	
16–21	**Country Backup, Carter Style**		DIX BRUCE
	19	*Worried Man Blues*	
	21	*Gold Watch and Chain*	
22–27	**Accompanying Your Voice**		ELIZABETH PAPAPETROU
	23	*Wildwood Flower*	
28–33	**Tackling Barre Chords**		JOHN GRIBBLE
	33	*Down in the Valley*	
34–39	**Moving Bass Lines**		HAPPY TRAUM
	37	*The Water Is Wide*	
	39	*Mr. Bojangles*	
40–46	**Using a Capo**		DAVID HAMBURGER
47–56	**Rock Rhythm**		DAVID HAMBURGER
57–64	**Chord Embellishment**		DYLAN SCHORER
	61–62	*Star of the County Down*	
	63–64	*June Apple*	

introduction

The acoustic guitar has found its way into virtually every style of music and has filled every conceivable musical role. Probably the most common function of the acoustic guitar, and the role that most of us begin with, is that of an accompaniment instrument. All you need are a few easily fingered chords and you're accompanying your voice on your favorite folk songs, backing up your roommate's fiddle or mandolin, or thrashing away in a rock 'n' roll frenzy. But once you've caught the bug, and you want to do a little more than furiously strum those C, G, D, A, or E chords, you'll be wanting to give your fingers a little something more to do.

In this book we take a look at the guitar's accompaniment role using both fingerpicking and flatpicking techniques in a number of different styles, including folk, rock, blues, Celtic, and bluegrass. Here are nine in-depth basic lessons from the master teachers at *Acoustic Guitar* magazine, with examples and songs that allow you to immediately apply your newly learned techniques. Be sure to check the music notation key on page 6 if you're unfamiliar with any terms or techniques used in the lessons, and if you need to refresh your memory about how to play a particular chord, take a look at the chord library on page 60.

Scott Nygaard
Editor

music notation key

The music in this book is written in standard notation and tablature. Here's how to read it.

STANDARD NOTATION

Standard notation is written on a five-line staff. Notes are written in alphabetical order from A to G.

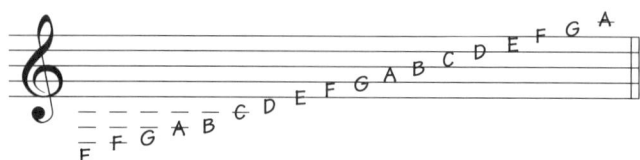

The duration of a note is determined by three things: the note head, stem, and flag. A whole note (o) equals four beats. A half note (♩) is half of that: two beats. A quarter note (♩) equals one beat, an eighth note (♪) equals half of one beat, and a 16th note (♬) is a quarter beat (there are four 16th notes per beat).

The fraction (4/4, 3/4, 6/8, etc.) or ¢ character shown at the beginning of a piece of music denotes the time signature. The top number tells you how many beats are in each measure, and the bottom number indicates the rhythmic value of each beat (4 equals a quarter note, 8 equals an eighth note, 16 equals a 16th note, and 2 equals a half note). The most common time signature is 4/4, which signifies four quarter notes per measure and is sometimes designated with the symbol c (for common time). The symbol ¢ stands for cut time (2/2). Most songs are either in 4/4 or 3/4.

TABLATURE

In tablature, the six horizontal lines represent the six strings of the guitar, with the first string on the top and sixth on the bottom. The numbers refer to fret numbers on a given string. The notation and tablature in this book are designed to be used in tandem—refer to the notation to get the rhythmic information and note durations, and refer to the tablature to get the exact locations of the notes on the guitar fingerboard.

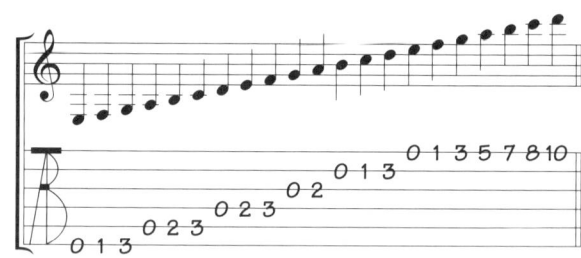

FINGERINGS

Fingerings are indicated with small numbers and letters in the notation. Fretting-hand fingering is indicated with 1 for the index finger, 2 the middle, 3 the ring, 4 the pinky, and *T* the thumb. Picking-hand fingering is indicated by *i* for the index finger, *m* the middle, *a* the ring, *c* the pinky, and *p* the thumb. Circled numbers indicate the string the note is played on. Remember that the fingerings indicated are only suggestions; if you find a different way that works better for you, use it.

CHORD DIAGRAMS

Chord diagrams show where the fingers go on the fingerboard. Frets are shown horizontally. The thick top line represents the nut. A Roman numeral to the right of a diagram indicates a chord played higher up the neck (in this case the top horizontal line is thin). Strings are shown as vertical lines. The line on the far left represents the sixth (lowest) string, and the line on the far right represents the first (highest) string. Dots show where the fingers go, and thick horizontal lines indicate barres. Numbers above the diagram are left-hand finger numbers, as used in standard notation. Again, the fingerings are only suggestions. An *X* indicates a string that should be muted or not played; 0 indicates an open string.

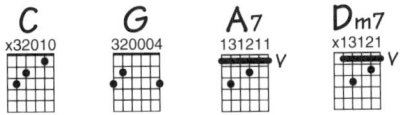

CAPOS

If a capo is used, a Roman numeral indicates the fret where the capo should be placed. The standard notation and tablature is written as if the capo were the nut of the guitar. For instance, a tune capoed anywhere up the neck and played using key-of-G chord shapes and fingerings will be written in the key of G. Likewise, open strings held down by the capo are written as open strings.

TUNINGS

Alternate guitar tunings are given from the lowest (sixth) string to the highest (first) string. For instance, D A D G B E indicates standard tuning with the bottom string dropped to D. Standard notation for songs in alternate tunings always reflects the actual pitches of the notes. Arrows underneath tuning notes indicate strings that are altered from standard tuning and whether they are tuned up or down.

VOCAL TUNES

Vocal tunes are sometimes written with a fully tabbed-out introduction and a vocal melody with chord diagrams for the rest of the piece. The tab intro is usually your indication of which strum or fingerpicking pattern to use in the rest of the piece. The melody with lyrics underneath is the melody sung by the vocalist. Occasionally, smaller notes are written with the melody to indicate the harmony part sung by another vocalist. These are not to be confused with cue notes, which are small notes that indicate melodies that vary when a section is repeated. Listen to a recording of the piece to get a feel for the guitar accompaniment and to hear the singing if you aren't skilled at reading vocal melodies.

ARTICULATIONS

There are a number of ways you can articulate a note on the guitar. Notes connected with slurs (not to be confused with ties) in the tablature or standard notation are articulated with either a hammer-on, pull-off, or slide. Lower notes slurred to higher notes are played as hammer-ons; higher notes slurred to lower notes are played as pull-offs. While it's usually obvious that slurred notes are played as hammer-ons or pull-offs, an *H* or *P* is included above the tablature as an extra reminder.

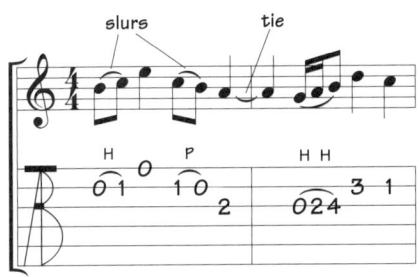

Slides are represented with a dash, and an *S* is included above the tab. A dash preceding a note represents a slide into the note from an indefinite point in the direction of the slide; a dash following a note indicates a slide off of the note to an indefinite point in the direction of the slide. For two slurred notes connected with a slide, you should pick the first note and then slide into the second.

Bends are represented with upward curves, as shown in the next example. Most bends have a specific destination pitch—the number above the bend symbol shows how much the bend raises the string's pitch: ¼ for a slight bend, ½ for a half step, 1 for a whole step.

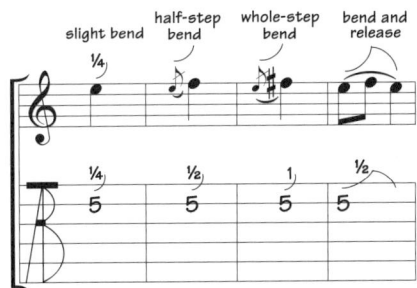

Grace notes are represented by small notes with a dash through the stem in standard notation and with small numbers in the tab. A grace note is a very quick ornament leading into a note, most commonly executed as a hammer-on, pull-off, or slide. In the first example below, pluck the note at the fifth fret on the beat, then quickly hammer onto the seventh fret. The second example is executed as a quick pull-off from the second fret to the open string. In the third example, both notes at the fifth fret are played simultaneously (even though it appears that the fifth fret, fourth string, is to be played by itself), then the seventh fret, fourth string, is quickly hammered.

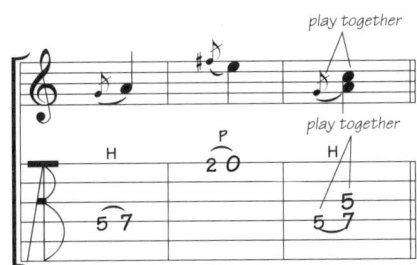

HARMONICS

Harmonics are represented by diamond-shaped notes in the standard notation and a small dot next to the tablature numbers. Natural harmonics are indicated with the text "Harmonics" or "Harm." above the tablature. Harmonics articulated with the right hand (often called artificial harmonics) include the text "R.H. Harmonics" or "R.H. Harm." above the tab. Right-hand harmonics are executed by lightly touching the harmonic node (usually 12 frets above the open string or fretted note) with the right-hand index finger and plucking the string with the thumb or ring finger or pick. For extended phrases played with right-hand harmonics, the fretted notes are shown in the tab along with instructions to touch the harmonics 12 frets above the notes.

REPEATS

One of the most confusing parts of a musical score can be the navigation symbols, such as repeats, *D.S. al Coda*, *D.C. al Fine*, *To Coda*, etc.

Repeat symbols are placed at the beginning and end of the passage to be repeated.

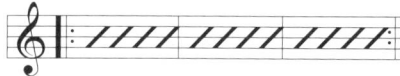

You should ignore repeat symbols with the dots on the right side the first time you encounter them; when you come to a repeat symbol with dots on the left side, jump back to the previous repeat symbol facing the opposite direction (if there is no previous symbol, go to the beginning of the piece). The next time you come to the repeat symbol, ignore it and keep going unless it includes instructions such as "Repeat three times."

A section will often have a different ending after each repeat. The example below includes a first and a second ending. Play until you hit the repeat symbol, jump back to the previous repeat symbol and play until you reach the bracketed first ending, skip the measures under the bracket and jump immediately to the second ending, and then continue.

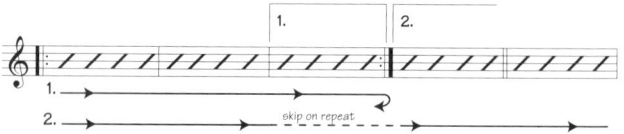

D.S. stands for *dal segno* or "from the sign." When you encounter this indication, jump immediately to the sign (𝄋). *D.S.* is usually accompanied by *al Fine* or *al Coda*. *Fine* indicates the end of a piece. A coda is a final passage near the end of a piece and is indicated with ⊕. *D.S. al Coda* simply tells you to jump back to the sign and continue on until you are instructed to jump to the coda, indicated with *To Coda* ⊕.

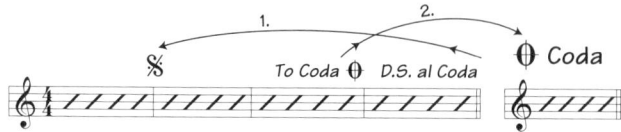

D.C. stands for *da capo* or "from the beginning." Jump to the top of the piece when you encounter this indication.

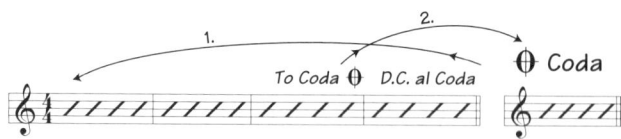

D.C. al Fine tells you to jump to the beginning of a tune and continue until you encounter the *Fine* indicating the end of the piece (ignore the *Fine* the first time through).

about the teachers

DIX BRUCE

Dix Bruce is a musician, composer, and writer from the San Francisco Bay Area. Mel Bay has published over 30 of his instructional books, videos, and recordings on subjects ranging from traditional country music to swing and jazz, and Bruce has also written for *Acoustic Guitar, Frets, The Fretted Instrument Guild of America,* and *Flatpicking Guitar.* Bruce has recorded two CDs of traditional and original acoustic guitar and vocal music with guitarist Jim Nunally and has also released two solo CDs, one of traditional American music, the other of string swing and jazz (all on Musix, PO Box 231005, Pleasant Hill, CA 94523).

JOHN GRIBBLE

John Gribble has taught thousands of people to play guitar. He was active as a guitar teacher in southern California for over 25 years and has taught in a variety of situations. For many years he was a judge at the renowned Topanga Banjo and Fiddle Contest and was the guitar workshop coordinator at the Summer Solstice Folk Music and Dance Festival, put on by the California Traditional Music Society. He currently lives in Tokyo, Japan, and divides his time between teaching music privately, teaching English at the Tokyo National University of Music and Fine Art, and writing.

DAVID HAMBURGER

David Hamburger is a guitarist, teacher, and writer who lives in Brooklyn, New York. He plays guitar, Dobro, and pedal steel on his 1994 debut recording, *King of the Brooklyn Delta* (Chester Records, PO Box 170504, Brooklyn, NY 11217), and on many other artists' recordings, including Chuck Brodsky's *Letters in the Dirt* (Red House, 1996). Hamburger is a regular teacher at the National Guitar Summer Workshop and author of several instruction books.

ELIZABETH PAPAPETROU

Elizabeth Papapetrou is a singer-songwriter, guitarist, and recording engineer who also designs Web pages and runs a Web resource company called Motherheart (gnv.fdt.net/~mother/). Originally from the U.K. and now living in Florida, she has been writing for music magazines for more than 17 years.

DYLAN SCHORER

Dylan Schorer was *Acoustic Guitar*'s music editor from 1994 to 1999. He won the 1993 fingerpicking contest at the Telluride Bluegrass Festival, and he performs throughout the San Francisco Bay Area, accompanying various songwriters and playing solo. He currently plays and records in the Celtic ensemble Logan's Well with guitarist Steve Baughman and vocalist Carleen Duncan.

JANET SMITH

Janet Smith has been been writing and performing acoustic music for many years. She has played at numerous festivals, recorded for Takoma Records, and taught guitar both privately and at Merritt College in Oakland, California. She was *Acoustic Guitar* magazine's music copyist and engraver for four years, and her transcriptions and copy work includes books for Stefan Grossman's Guitar Workshop and Centerstream Publishing. Her beginning fingerpicking guitar instruction book and cassette *Fingerstyle Guitar Solos* is distributed by Hal Leonard.

HAPPY TRAUM

For more than 35 years, Happy Traum has been a major influence in the world of folk and traditional music, recording numerous albums, both solo and with distinguished groups such as the New World Singers. He has also accompanied other famous musicians, such as Bob Dylan. As the founder (with his wife, Jane Traum) and president of Homespun Tapes, Traum has contributed significantly to music instruction for more than 30 years, compiling a library of approximately 400 different music lessons on various media. His lesson "Folk Song Accompaniment" in this book is based on the instructional video *Creating Folk Song Arrangements* (Homespun Tapes, PO Box 694, Woodstock, NY 12498; [800] 33-TAPES).

GETTING STARTED

Folk Song Accompaniment
Happy Traum

The acoustic guitar is the most popular instrument in the world today. One of the reasons for this is that with a little help from a good teacher or some instructional materials, you can make music the first time you pick up a guitar. All you need are two chords and a little strumming to accompany yourself on dozens of songs; once you have three chords, you can play thousands of tunes. If that's all you are inclined to do, you can stop there and still get satisfaction playing for yourself and your friends.

If you want to take your playing to the next level, though, you can achieve some wonderful effects without great technical virtuosity. There are many small touches that can absolutely transform a song, turning even the simplest two-chord melody into a true performance piece. All it takes is a little extra knowledge, a few tricks of the trade, and (of course) some practice.

Here are some easy techniques from which you can pick and choose to create your own unique arrangements. The ones you decide to use will reflect your particular taste and musical inclinations, and hopefully you will then apply these ideas to other songs, in other keys. When you can do that, you'll be on your way to becoming a real guitarist.

To illustrate these techniques, I have chosen the wonderful old cowboy song "Down in the Valley." It's one of those two-chord pieces that I would teach to a brand-new player on his or her first lesson. On page 12 you'll find the song in its most basic form.

This song is in 3/4 (waltz) time: 1-2-3, 1-2-3. Here's one of my favorite picking patterns for this meter:

Introduction

There are many small touches that can absolutely transform a song.

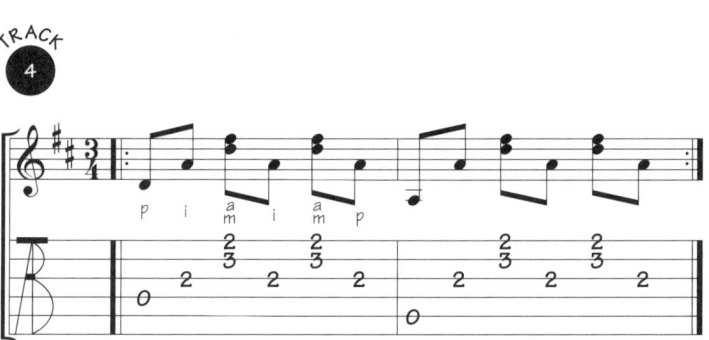

Note that in this kind of picking, your thumb plays the bass strings (fourth, fifth, and sixth), while your index, middle, and ring fingers are each assigned one of the treble strings: the third, second, and first, respectively. If you haven't used this type of right-hand picking before, you may need some practice. Try to keep your hand and wrist fairly still, moving only your fingers. Pluck perpendicularly to the strings, so you get as clear a sound as possible. It's helpful to have slightly long fingernails on your right hand to help catch the strings and create a good, sharp tone.

Down in the Valley

Traditional, arranged by Happy Traum

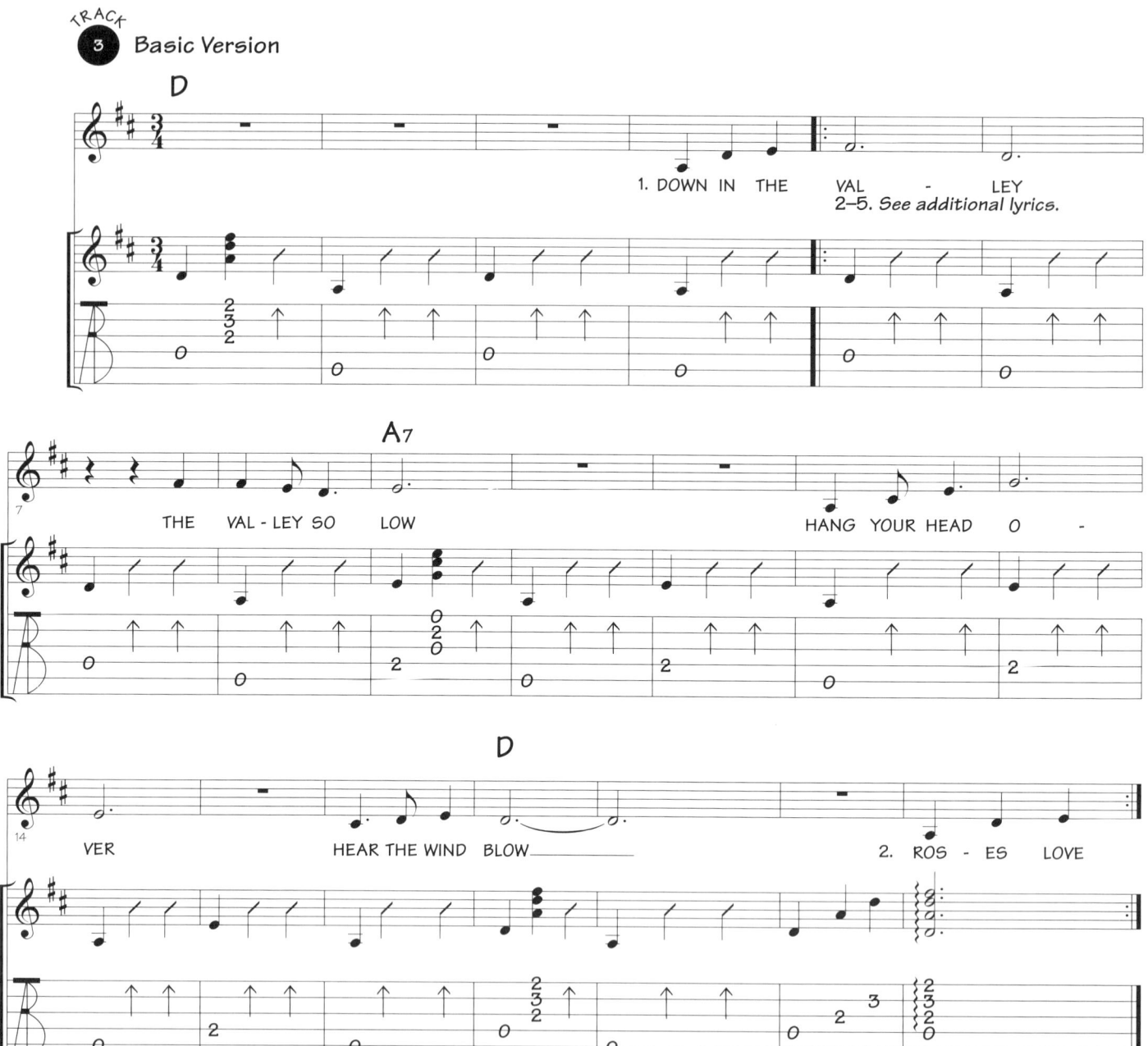

1. DOWN IN THE VALLEY, VALLEY SO LOW
   HANG YOUR HEAD OVER HEAR THE WIND BLOW

2. ROSES LOVE SUNSHINE VIOLETS LOVE DEW
   ANGELS IN HEAVEN KNOW I LOVE YOU
   KNOW I LOVE YOU DEAR KNOW I LOVE YOU
   ANGELS IN HEAVEN KNOW I LOVE YOU

3. IF YOU DON'T LOVE ME LOVE WHOM YOU PLEASE
   THROW YOUR ARMS 'ROUND ME GIVE MY HEART EASE
   GIVE MY HEART EASE LOVE GIVE MY HEART EASE
   THROW YOUR ARMS 'ROUND ME GIVE MY HEART EASE

4. BUILD ME A CASTLE FORTY FEET HIGH
   SO I CAN SEE HIM AS HE RIDES BY
   AS HE RIDES BY LOVE AS HE RIDES BY
   SO I CAN SEE HIM AS HE RIDES BY

5. WRITE ME A LETTER SEND IT BY MAIL
   SEND IT IN CARE OF BIRMINGHAM JAIL
   BIRMINGHAM JAIL LOVE BIRMINGHAM JAIL
   SEND IT IN CARE OF BIRMINGHAM JAIL

Now back to the song. Here are some ways to spruce up your performance.

Easy hint No. 1: the D6 chord. This chord, which is used a lot in jazz and pop music, also gives you a sound that is almost a cliché in popularized songs of the old west. It's easy! All you have to do is lift up your third finger, allowing the open second string (the sixth note of the scale: B) to ring out. You'll get a really nice effect, especially using this 3/4 strum. Now try "Down in the Valley" again, occasionally substituting the D6 chord for the D chord.

Easy hint No. 2: the A7sus4 chord. This one definitely sounds more complicated than it is. The sus4 (short for *suspended fourth*) chord simply adds the fourth note of the scale to the rest of the chord, which gives it a suspended or hanging feeling. Because of this, it is always used as a passing chord, resolving to the regular A7.

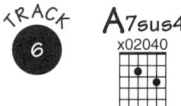

Easy hint No. 3: the Em7. You probably know the simple Em chord. If you add the D note, using your pinky finger on the second string, third fret, it becomes an Em7. (Note that your pinky is playing the same note you used to turn the A7 into a sus4 chord.) Try substituting Em7 for A7 on the word *low* in "Down in the Valley" (measure 9).

Since the melody note at this point in the song is an E, and there is an E in both Em7 and A7, it should work nicely. It also creates interest and movement in a part of the song in which we've been playing just one chord for eight measures. You can try this same chord substitution in the next line, starting with the word *over* (measure 13). The embellished version of "Down in the Valley" on page 14 utilizes all of these substitutions.

There are many other songs that you can arrange this way, but it will take some practice before you can easily hear where these substitute chords can be added. In time, though, and with some experimentation, you'll find that you'll be enriching your repertoire and surprising your listeners with lovely arrangements of even the most basic material.

Down in the Valley

Traditional, arranged by Happy Traum

Now we'll see what other tools are available to us in building an accompaniment for "Down in the Valley." Let's insert some bass runs, which will add movement as well as a harmony line to the melody. We can put one right into the pickup, the notes leading into the downbeat on the first syllable of the word *valley*. You can simply go up the scale from your bass A note. Remember that when you reach the D (the fourth note of the run), you are into your waltz-time picking pattern. Try putting the same bass run into the last line as well, on the words *hear the wind blow*.

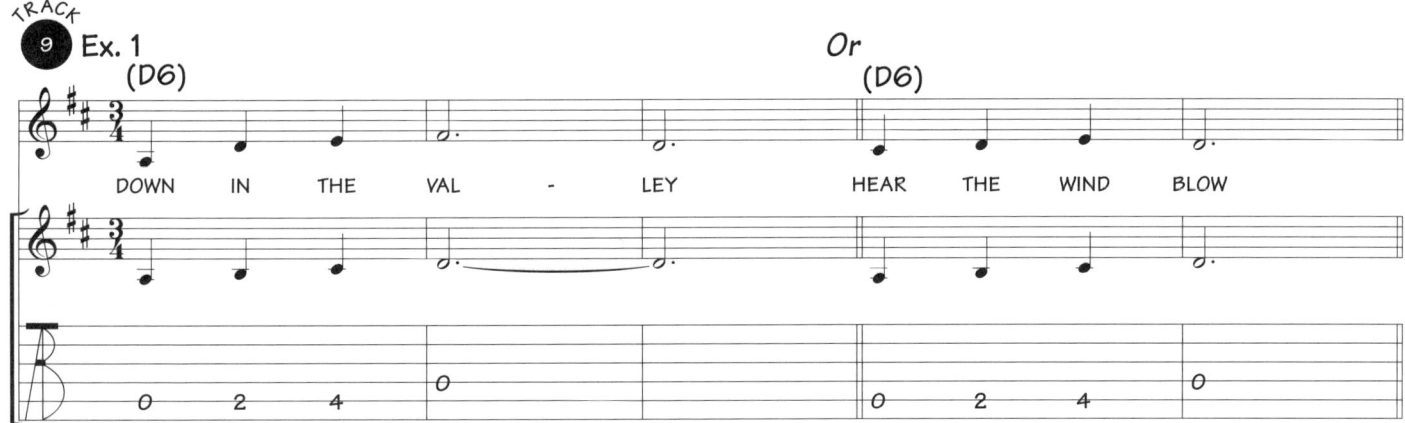

You can also add a bass run when you change from D to A7, on the words *valley so low*. This time go down the scale from D to A. If you decide you want to use the Em7 instead of A7, as I suggested earlier, just play the low E as your last note. Here it is both ways:

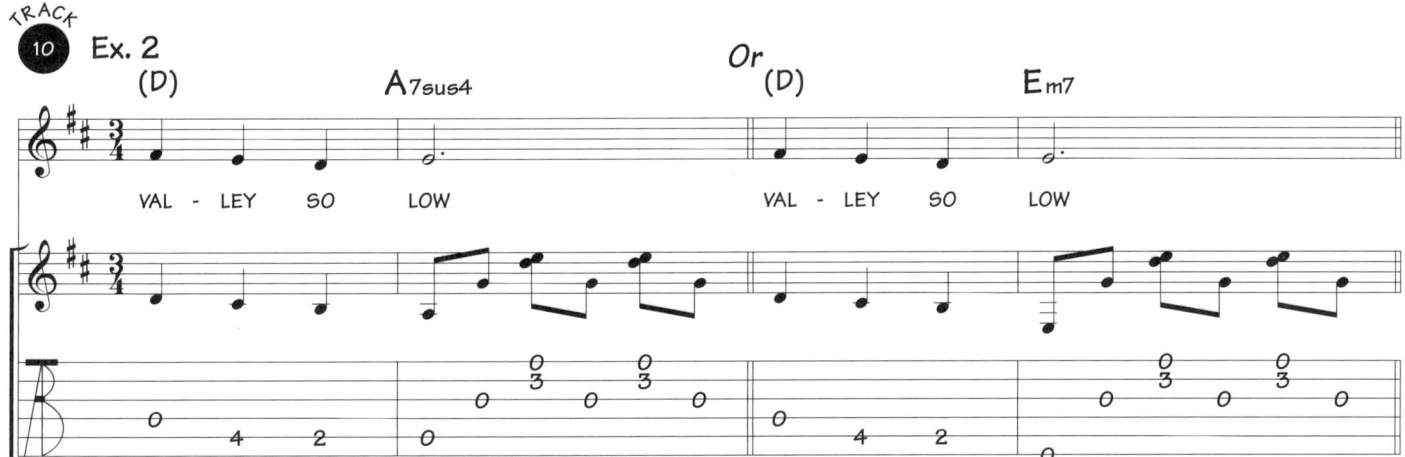

We can add additional interest to this arrangement by putting in a turnaround. This can be a chord progression or a series of single notes that bring you around to the beginning of the next verse. Let's try a progression that simply goes from D to G to A7. (In the key of D, the A7 chord leads your ear back to the tonic, or D chord.)

Let's put some bass runs into the turnaround now. Because each chord is only played for one measure, we have less time to get those bass notes in, so we have to play them as eighth notes instead of quarter notes (two notes for each beat instead of one). Notice also that we have to break up the right-hand strum in order to fit the bass notes in.

You can vary your right-hand pattern by adding extra bass notes, which will also create movement and interest. Simply substitute a bass note for the little two-note chord on the next-to-last beat of the measure:

Finally, you might want to play an instrumental version of this tune (Example 6). The easiest way to accomplish this is to play the melody in the bass, while keeping the picking going as much as possible.

GETTING STARTED

The only tricky thing here is that the melody goes to an F# (fourth string, fourth fret) while you're holding down a D chord. Here's a new position for that chord. This may take a bit of practicing, but it'll be worth it. This position will come in handy in future arrangements.

Notice that on the part of the melody where you sing the word *over,* you have to somehow get a G note while keeping the picking pattern going over an Em chord. The easiest way to do this is to simply play the fourth string at the fifth fret (a G note) while continuing to pluck the open three strings above it (measure 9). (When you play the Em chord in its basic position, you normally keep the first three strings open. This is essentially the same thing, with a different note in the bass.) I use my pinky finger to get this note, but you can also use your ring finger if that's more comfortable for you.

Well that's about it for this song. You now have a complete arrangement, both for soloing and accompaniment. Not bad for a relative beginner! There's lots more you can do with this song, and I encourage you to experiment as much as possible, using different bass notes, picking patterns, strums, arpeggios, and other variations.

GETTING STARTED

Country Backup, Carter Style
Dix Bruce

Virtually every bluegrass and traditional country guitarist uses this accompaniment technique.

Introduction

Few names are more important in the history of American old-time and country music than the Carter Family of Virginia. Through their recordings, beginning in 1927, they popularized a vast repertoire of mountain music and styles of vocal and instrumental performance that continue to influence modern folk, bluegrass, and traditional country styles.

The songs of the Carter Family, many written or collected by A.P. Carter, are classics: "Can the Circle Be Unbroken?" "Diamonds in the Rough," "Wildwood Flower," "Bury Me under the Weeping Willow," "I'm Thinking Tonight of My Blue Eyes," "Keep on the Sunny Side," "Gold Watch and Chain," "Midnight on the Stormy Deep," and many more. Sara Carter's direct and unpretentious lead singing set a standard for honest country delivery. Maybelle Carter's distinctive guitar and Autoharp styles were perfectly suited to a small vocal group in which she was often the only instrumentalist. With her Gibson L-5 archtop, she provided the perfect accompaniment to the trio's singing and developed an approach to lead playing that combined single-string melodies with chord strums. The term *Carter picking* was coined to describe her playing, which effectively allowed her solo guitar to sound like more than one instrument—both rhythm and lead.

"Worried Man Blues," an old Carter Family song that was revived during the folk music craze of the early 1960s, illustrates the basic backup guitar style Mother Maybelle used. Virtually every bluegrass and traditional country guitarist uses this technique. As the example below shows, it is based on picking a bass note on the downbeats (the 1 and 3 of a 1 2 3 4 measure) and strumming a chord on the backbeats (the 2 and 4 of the measure). Here's what this pattern looks like written out:

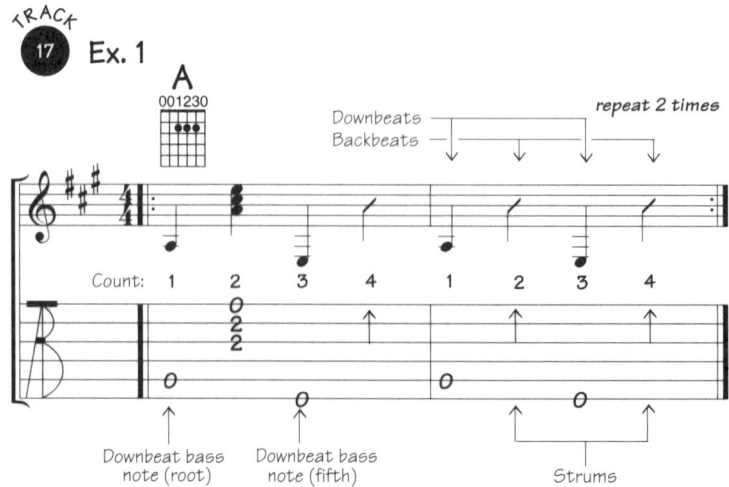

The bass note on beat 1, a downbeat, is the *root tone* of the chord. This note has the same letter name as the chord: the root of the A chord is an A note, etc. The bass note on beat 3, also a downbeat, is usually the fifth of the chord. This note is five scale steps up from the root of the chord: in the case of the A chord, the fifth scale step is an E note (A is the root, B is the second, C is the third, D is the fourth, and E is the fifth), which we play with the open sixth string. On some chords, like G or C, the third of the chord might be used as a bass note instead of the fifth. The following example shows where the root and fifth are on all three chords used in "Worried Man Blues."

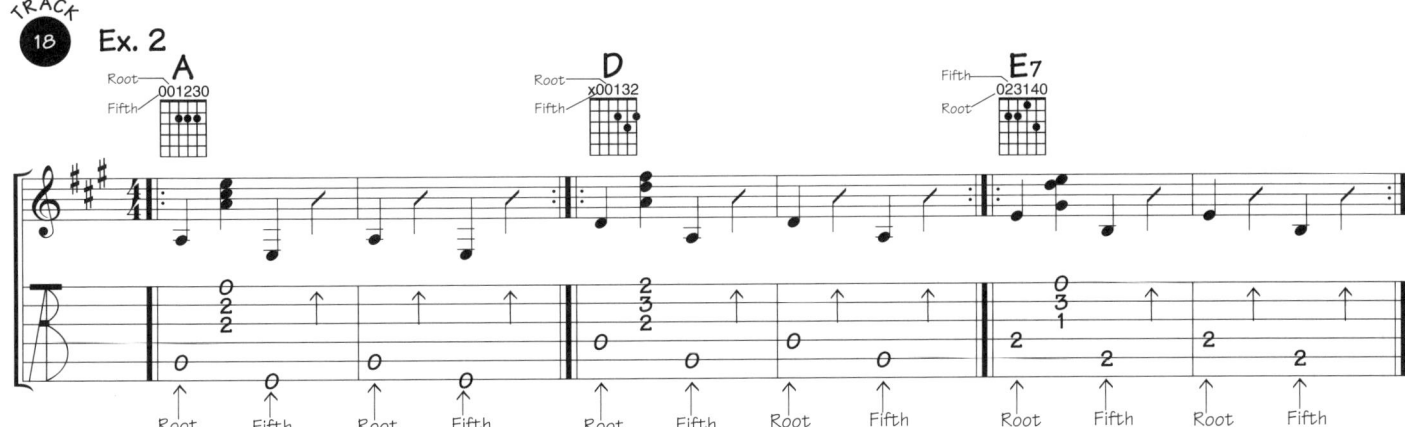

Practice these patterns along with the CD to familiarize yourself with the bass note locations before you try the whole song.

The first verse of this song has straight bass-and-strum backup. Use all downstrokes and work for an even, controlled feel on both the bass notes and the strums. Mother Maybelle used a thumbpick for bass notes and her fingers for strums, but I suggest using a flatpick, as it's a bit more controllable when you graduate to more complex single-string picking. You may find that you naturally give the backbeats (strums) a bit more accent or volume; make sure they don't overpower the bass notes.

The second verse adds some possibilities for connecting the chords with bass runs. A number next to a note head indicates which left-hand finger to use to fret that note: 1 for the index, 2 for the middle, 3 for the ring, and 4 for the little finger. Keep the timing even and straight. Jump right in and try your own licks too, and don't forget to write them down for future reference.

Be sure to play through all the verses to "Worried Man Blues." Practice the backup until you don't have to think about it. Keep in mind that you're not just memorizing one tune, you're working on the basic moves you'll need for every song you play in this style. These basic moves out of open chords like the A, D, and E lead directly to more advanced solo picking, especially Mother Maybelle's "Carter-style" leads.

"Gold Watch and Chain" is another one of my favorite Carter Family songs. It's simple, it's pretty, and it does an admirable job of describing the heartbreak of lost love. It's a bit more challenging to play than "Worried Man Blues," but along the way you will more than double your experience with Carter-style backup and learn bass note/strum patterns on four more chords.

RECOMMENDED LISTENING

You can hear this basic style of backup on just about any traditional country recording. Rounder Records has reissued all the recordings the Carter Family made for Victor from 1927 to 1941 on nine CDs. The set is a treasure trove of excellent music, wonderful songs, and beautiful guitar playing. Both "Worried Man Blues" and "Gold Watch and Chain" are included in this series; they actually name the CDs they're on. I recorded "Gold Watch and Chain" with Tom Rozum on a CD called **My Folk Heart** (Musix, PO Box 231005, Pleasant Hill, CA 94523; musix1@aol.com). Arhoolie Records has also issued three CDs of live Carter Family performances (**On Border Radio,** Vols. 1–3) from radio station XET in 1939 that feature most of the songs the Carters made famous, plus many lesser-known gems by A.P. Carter and assorted Carter children. Though the individual cuts were shortened in performance to fit the format of the old radio programs, they're a great collection nonetheless.

Listen to recordings by Doc Watson, Tony Rice, the Monroe Brothers, and Ricky Skaggs as well as Norman Blake and Tony Rice for other examples of great backup and lead acoustic guitar playing. You might also enjoy my duo recordings with Jim Nunally, which demonstrate the same backup concepts discussed in this lesson.

Worried Man Blues

Words and music by A.P. Carter, Maybelle Carter, and Sara Carter; arranged by Dix Bruce

© 1930, copyright renewed, by Peer International Corp. International copyright secured. All rights reserved.

GETTING STARTED

IT TAKES A WORRIED MAN
TO SING A WORRIED SONG
IT TAKES A WORRIED MAN
TO SING A WORRIED SONG
I'M WORRIED NOW
BUT I WON'T BE WORRIED LONG

1. I WENT ACROSS THE RIVER
   AND I LAY DOWN TO SLEEP
   I WENT ACROSS THE RIVER
   AND I LAY DOWN TO SLEEP
   WHEN I AWOKE
   I HAD SHACKLES ON MY FEET

   CHORUS

2. TWENTY-NINE LINKS
   OF CHAIN AROUND MY LEG
   TWENTY-NINE LINKS
   OF CHAIN AROUND MY LEG
   AND ON EACH LINK
   AN INITIAL OF MY NAME

   CHORUS

3. I ASKED THE JUDGE
   "WHAT MIGHT BE MY FINE?"
   I ASKED THE JUDGE
   "WHAT MIGHT BE MY FINE?"
   "TWENTY-ONE YEARS
   ON THE ROCKY MOUNTAIN LINE"

   CHORUS

4. IF ANYONE SHOULD ASK YOU
   WHO COMPOSED THIS SONG
   IF ANYONE SHOULD ASK YOU
   WHO COMPOSED THIS SONG
   TELL 'EM 'TWAS I
   AND I SING IT ALL DAY LONG

   CHORUS

We'll play "Gold Watch and Chain" in the key of G but we'll capo it up to the third fret. The resulting sound will be in the key of B♭, which is three half steps (one fret equals one half step) above the key of G. Example 3 shows the chords you'll use with their bass notes diagrammed.

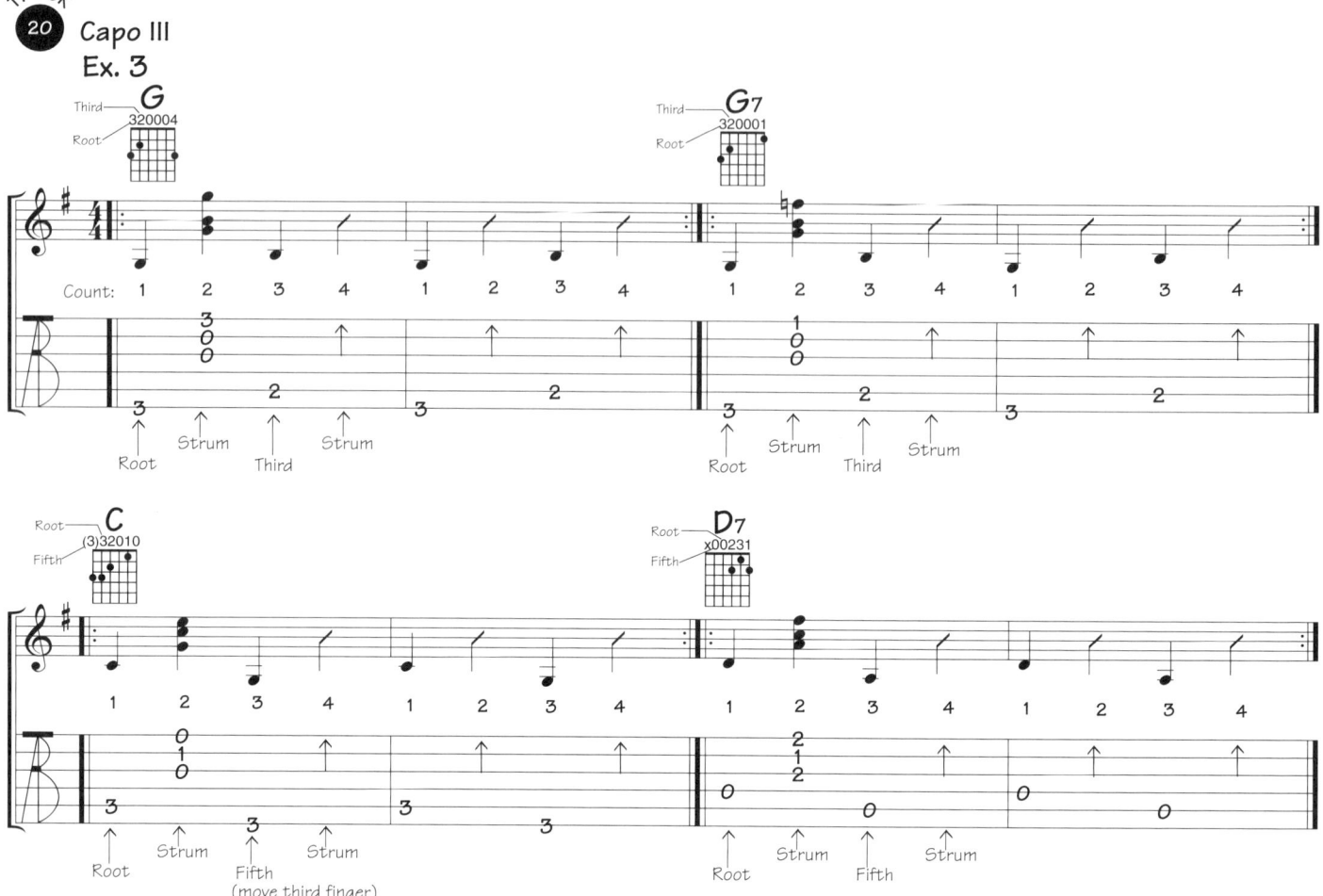

Practice the patterns along with the CD to familiarize yourself with the bass note locations.

You'll notice that the G and G7 chords use a root-strum/third-strum pattern instead of the root-strum/fifth-strum you learned previously. You could play a root-strum/fifth-strum pattern by substituting the open fourth-string D note (the fifth of the G chord) for the fifth-string B note (the third). Practice both ways.

On the C chord you'll need to move your third finger from the third fret of the fifth string (C or root) to the third fret of the sixth string (G or fifth). This will take some practice to coordinate if you're not used to doing it. Play it slowly at first, making sure that your rhythm is even and that you don't speed up and slow down as you change bass notes. Play each bass note cleanly and clearly.

Singing along while you play will make it a lot more fun. The melody is included for those of you who are not familiar with the tune. Don't be shy—nobody has to hear but you. One more suggestion: if you aren't already getting together and jamming with other players, start today. You'll learn much faster by sharing.

GETTING STARTED

Gold Watch and Chain
Words and music by A.P. Carter, arranged by Dix Bruce

© 1960, copyright renewed, by Peer International Corp. International copyright secured. All rights reserved.

1. DARLING HOW CAN I STAY HERE WITHOUT YOU?
   WHEN I'VE NOTHING TO CHEER MY POOR HEART
   THIS OLD WORLD WILL BE SAD DEAR WITHOUT YOU
   TELL ME NOW THAT WE'RE NEVER TO PART

   OH I'LL PAWN YOU MY GOLD WATCH AND CHAIN LOVE
   AND I'LL PAWN YOU MY GOLD DIAMOND RING
   I WILL PAWN YOU THIS HEART IN MY BOSOM
   ONLY SAY THAT YOU LOVE ME AGAIN

2. TAKE BACK ALL THE GIFTS YOU HAVE GIVEN
   A DIAMOND RING AND A LOCK OF YOUR HAIR
   AND A CARD WITH YOUR PICTURE UPON IT
   IT'S A FACE THAT IS FALSE BUT IT'S FAIR

   CHORUS

3. TELL ME WHY YOU DO NOT LOVE ME
   TELL ME WHY YOUR SMILE IS NOT RIGHT
   TELL ME WHY YOU HAVE GROWN SO DOWNHEARTED
   IS THERE NO KISS FOR ME LOVE TONIGHT

GETTING STARTED

Accompanying Your Voice
Elizabeth Papapetrou

I remember when I first tried to sing and play guitar at the same time: that weird feeling of floundering in uncoordinated cacophony as my body rebelled at the idea of doing too many things at once. I felt a bit like a kid on her first bicycle. I tried it again . . . and *again*. Same story.

So, why is learning these skills such a bugaboo? Well, let's take a look at everything you have to do to get it going. First off, just playing the guitar requires two hands doing independent dances at opposite ends of the fretboard. Then, singing means doing stuff that you might feel a little insecure about, involving body, mind, breath, and voice. Finally, there's the added complication of remembering words. It's a bit like that old coordination game of trying to rub your stomach while patting your head—but 100 times harder.

If that's not enough, we add to this the challenge of maintaining one rhythm on the guitar and overlaying it with a different vocal rhythm. And when we do get both things going at once, each skill is far less polished than it is on its own.

So, how do we learn to sing and play at the same time? The answer is practice and more practice and even more practice. That's the only thing that will get you to a place where you feel comfortable with yourself, your guitar, and your voice.

THE GUITAR PART

Begin with a simple, well-known, medium-paced acoustic song that uses a few standard-shaped chords that change infrequently and only on the first beat of a 4/4 bar. "Wildwood Flower," a traditional song best known as a great beginner's flatpicking tune, is a perfect example.

It's helpful to have a copy of any song you're learning on tape, CD, or record, preferably performed as you would like to play it. If you have a favorite version of "Wildwood Flower," you can listen to that, or listen to my version.

Begin by singing along with the recording, while holding your guitar in the position in which you normally play it. I highly recommend that you learn to play standing up, with a strap to hold your guitar, because we human beings sing much better standing up. If you just *have* to sit down, teach yourself to sit with your back and neck upright. It may feel cool to slouch over your guitar, but it adds one more obstruction to the flow of air in your throat.

So now you're singing along with the recording, holding your guitar, and beginning to feel comfortable with that. Remember that the key to every aspect of this process is practice, so stick to it and only move on when you really feel ready. Have patience! Now, try singing the same song unaccompanied, still holding your guitar with your back straight.

Learning to sing and play at the same time is like trying to rub your stomach while patting your head.

Introduction

Wildwood Flower

Traditional, arranged by Elizabeth Papapetrou

1. SHE'LL TWINE MID HER RINGLETS OF RAVEN BLACK HAIR
   THE LILIES SO PALE AND THE ROSES SO FAIR
   AND THE MYRTLE SO BRIGHT WITH AN EMERALD HUE
   AND THE PALE ARROWNETTA WITH EYES OF BRIGHT BLUE

2. HE TOLD HER HE LOVED HER AND CALLED HER HIS FLOWER
   THAT BLOSSOMED FOR HIM ALL THE BRIGHTER EACH HOUR
   THOUGH HER HEART NOW IS BREAKING, HE NEVER SHALL KNOW
   THAT HIS NAME MAKES HER TREMBLE, HER PALE CHEEKS TO GLOW

3. SHE'LL SING AND SHE'LL DANCE AND HER LAUGH SHALL BE GAY
   SHE'LL CHARM EVERY HEART AND THE CROWD SHE WILL SWAY
   SHE WILL LIVE YET TO SEE HIM REGRET THE DARK HOUR
   WHEN HE WON AND NEGLECTED THIS FRAIL WILDWOOD FLOWER

4. SHE'LL THINK OF HIM NEVER, SHE'LL BE WILD AND GAY
   SHE'LL CEASE THIS WILD WEEPING, DRIVE SORROW AWAY
   BUT SHE WAKES FROM HER DREAMING, HER IDOL WAS CLAY
   AND HER VISIONS OF LOVE HAVE ALL VANISHED AWAY

GETTING STARTED

Now try just playing the chords to "Wildwood Flower." Here's a basic strumming pattern you could use for this song.

TRACK 24 Ex. 1

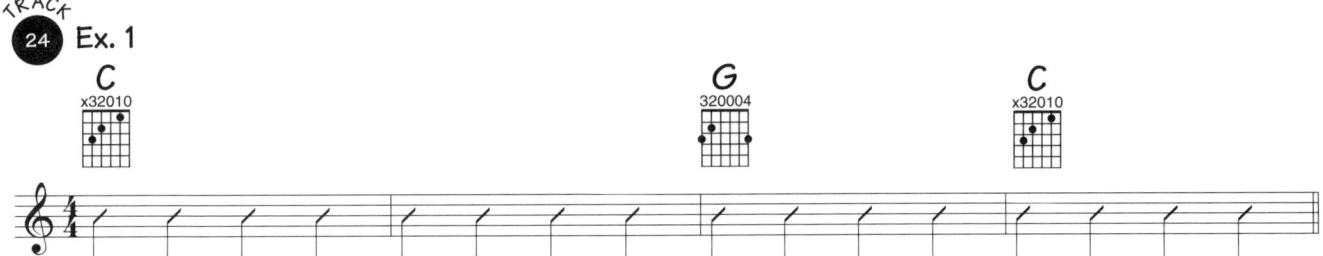

The more automatic the guitar part becomes for you, the easier it will be to add in the singing. Alternate between singing and holding your guitar and playing without singing. When you're sure you feel comfortable with both aspects, you're ready to put them together.

VOICE AND GUITAR TOGETHER

Keep your first efforts low-key and low-volume. Just go for it two or three times, as slow as feels comfortable. Remember that it isn't necessary for you to sound just like the writer or original performer of the song. Each artist has his or her own qualities to offer, and *different* doesn't mean better or worse. It may be that you're off and running straight away ("Look Ma! I'm doing it!"). If not, it will quickly become apparent where you need to do some work. The usual problems are forgetting the words and song structure, missing the changes, and/or losing the rhythm.

The problem may simply be that the words are tripping you up. Try playing the song again while whistling, humming, or wordlessly voicing the melody. Some folks find that this approach makes a huge difference, but others get confused and do worse. Another technique is playing the song while singing it in your head, i.e., imagining yourself singing the melody, with or without words. This a really useful skill to develop. When you begin recording songs, you may need to record the guitar and voice separately. If you're imagining the vocals while you're laying down the guitar part, the voice and guitar tend to blend better. It's also an easier way to keep track of the song's structure than counting bars while you play.

Or, it could be the melody that's putting you off. Play your guitar and say the words without melody, but in the correct rhythm.

Now try singing unaccompanied and then add guitar, beginning by only strumming once on each chord change.

TRACK 25 Ex. 2

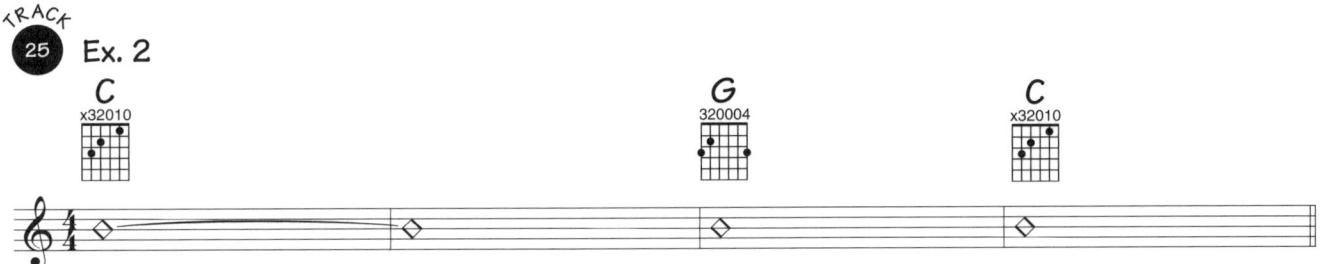

Next, strum only on the first beat of each measure.

TRACK 26 Ex. 3

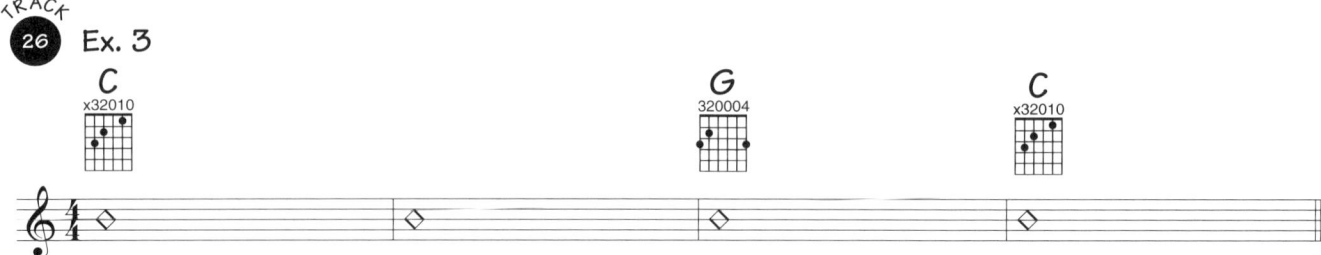

Then gradually add in the rest.

If you feel that maintaining rhythm is a problem, slow things down further. Playing much slower than usual gives you more time and space to move your fingers and place the words correctly. It also allows you to really hear what is going on and shine up your technique.

The example below shows a simple version of the melody for the adventurous among you who want to try your hands at singing and picking at the same time.

TRACK 27 Ex. 4

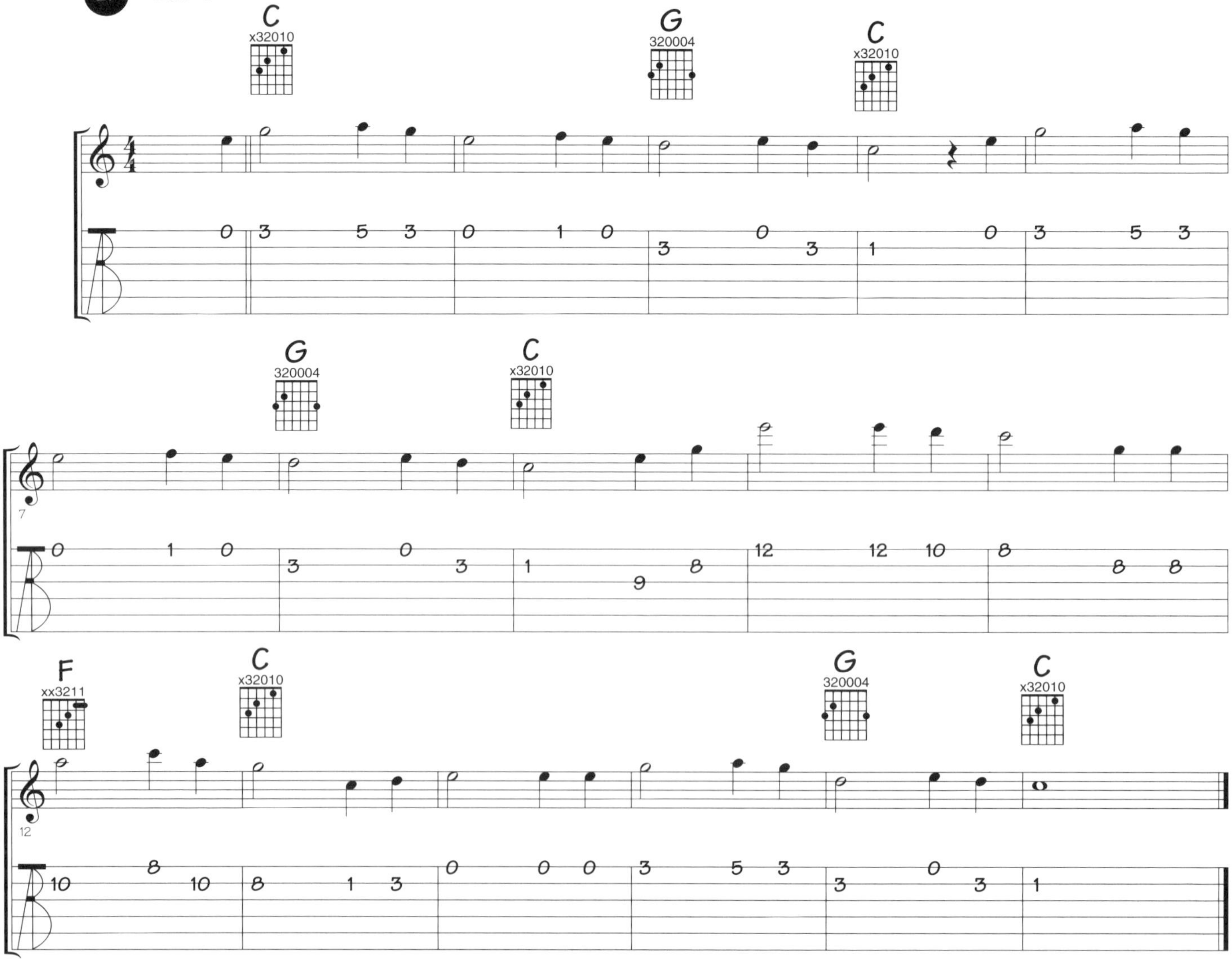

Again, practice is everything. The more you practice the easier it all becomes. Eventually, the playing and singing become so automatic that you have time to vary the vocal or guitar part. This discovery of freedom of expression is so exhilarating—it's like flying. Go for it!

GETTING STARTED

Speeding Up Chord Changes
Janet Smith

One of the many things that frustrate beginning guitar players is the extra time needed to change chords. Your fingers have just begun to get some calluses, the terrible buzzing sounds are starting to subside, and now you want to begin singing and playing a simple song. But darn it, it takes too long to get from one chord to another, and the music still won't flow smoothly!

We've all been there, and even though chord changes eventually get smoother as you gain experience, the early stages can drag on forever. Here are some typical bad habits that beginners need to eliminate in order to change chords more rapidly, along with remedies for these problems and a few other general tips for smoother playing.

Bad habit No. 1: You play fast right up until the last beat of a chord but slow down while changing and then allow the song and accompaniment to lurch forward at a furious pace after you strum the new chord.

Remedy: Play very slowly and evenly at this stage in your learning to eliminate some of the unmusical rush-and-wait effect. Strum or pluck the new chord after all the left-hand fingers are placed and continue slowly, without speeding up between changes. Rest between songs if necessary. Playing slowly is hard, because at slow tempos your left-hand fingers have to press down on the strings for a longer period of time than at faster speeds.

Bad habit No. 2: You halt the flow of music right before the chord change by slapping down on all the strings with your right hand.

Remedy: Do not damp the strings before each chord change. Let them ring out to fill in the gap between chords. As the pause between chords diminishes with practice, keep trying to sustain the feel and continuity of the song from one chord to the next. Focus on the feel of the music as soon as you can in your practicing sessions. Forgive the occasional buzzing string when you are concentrating on changing chords smoothly.

Bad habit No. 3: You rotate the guitar up to see the neck better and then rotate it forward again after the chord is finally in place.

Remedy: Hold the guitar so you can barely see the neck, just enough to place your left-hand fingers without rotating the guitar back and forth for each new chord. Looking at the neck of the guitar while you play is not necessarily bad, particularly if you're an instrumental soloist, but this habit can get in the way of a vocal performance. The audience wants to see a singer's face and hear the words clearly. If you want to sing as you play, practice looking out front instead of at your left hand. Standing up makes it almost impossible to see the neck of the guitar. If you want to play standing up, as on a stage or when strolling, you should spend part of your practice time doing just that, possibly in front of a mirror.

Bad habit No. 4: You form a new chord by putting your fingers down one at a time, starting from the highest string and working toward the bass.

Remedy: Play the bass note of the new chord first, making sure that it's on the proper beat and that you're not pausing beforehand. Only one left-hand finger (or sometimes none) is required for this one new note, so you can play it without waiting to find all the

These techniques will help you smooth out the flow of your accompaniment parts.

other fingers in the chord. Be sure to use the correct finger on the bass note for the upcoming chord position. Only after you play the bass should you take time to place the rest of your fingers in their proper positions. If the new chord has an open-string bass, so much the better. Just play the open string while you are positioning your other fingers.

Here's an example of how this technique works, in the song "Tom Dooley."

Practicing these techniques for speeding up chord changes will introduce you to other generally useful techniques. Playing an open bass string while changing chords, for instance, is standard practice. The bass note is usually the first note played in a chord, so fingering the bass first in the left hand is always a good idea. Whether playing slow or fast, alone or in a group, keeping an even tempo is a skill every musician must have. Slapping or stopping all the strings has a jarring, percussive effect, which can be useful if created intentionally but should not automatically be a part of every chord change. Except when creating special rhythmic effects, letting the strings ring out at the end of a piece is more effective than cutting the sound short. A good performance allows the magic of the music to fade naturally after the last note has been played.

When these new techniques for changing chords begin to take shape, it is time to work toward placing all the fingers of a chord simultaneously. To achieve this goal, shape a chord on the fretboard and slowly decrease the pressure of your fingers, lifting your hand slightly off the fretboard while retaining the chord's shape. Suspend the hand briefly above the neck, then replace it on the fingerboard, retaining the correct position of the fingers. Practice keeping the fingers from separating out of the chord configuration as they leave the neck of the guitar. Gradually increase the distance between the chording hand and the fretboard (over several days) until you can bring the hand up to the fretboard from any distance and place all fingers of the chord at once. This is an important skill that will help take you up to an intermediate level.

Tackling Barre Chords
John Gribble

Introduction

Barre chords are more an issue of technique than testosterone, and the technique is not difficult to learn.

Many beginning and intermediate guitarists are terrified of chords that require barring—placing the first finger across all six strings. They figure it takes the hands of a strangler to mash all six strings down at once and that they're never going to get it. The fact is, barre chords are more an issue of technique than testosterone, and the technique is not difficult to learn. Assuming your guitar's action (string height) is fairly low, you should be able to zip up and down the neck without much trouble in a very short time. What follows is a learning approach based on ideas from noted guitar teacher and writer Bob Baxter, which many students have found useful.

First, lose the idea that you have to press down all six strings at the same time and make them sound good. Unless you're in an open tuning, you don't. True, if you are playing a lovely arpeggio, you don't want *ping-ping-THUNK-ping,* but if you're banging out yet another chorus of "Wild Thing," who's going to notice if the second string is a little muted? And other fingers are usually there to do part of the job. Look at the barred F chord and the E chord below:

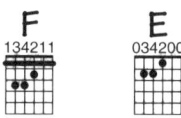

In the F chord, the third, fourth, and fifth strings are all covered by fingers other than the one doing the barre. To start, fret the E chord at right as shown. Note that the fingering is a little different than usual. You put your middle finger on the third string, first fret; your ring finger on the fifth string, second fret; and your pinky on the fourth string, second fret.

Check out Example 1:

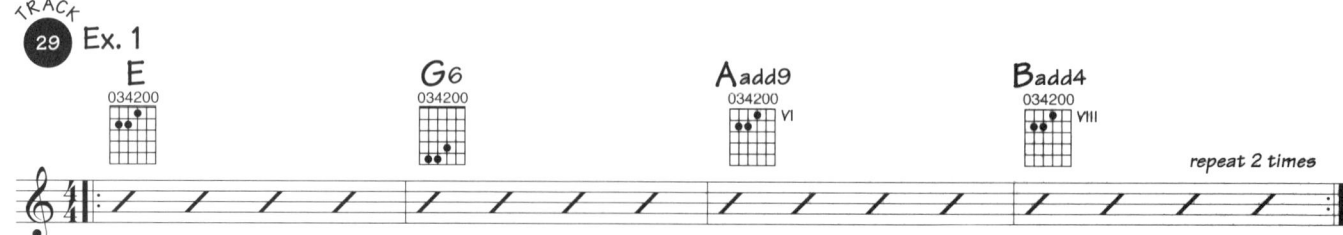

Fret that E and play a simple rhythm pattern, strumming down on the beat. Keep strumming and slide the whole chord up the neck (toward the guitar's body) so that your middle finger is at the fourth fret and your ring and pinky fingers are both on the fifth fret. You may have to loosen your fingers a little to make the slide, but don't take them all the way off the strings. You're now playing a very nice G6. Next, slide your hand up two more frets, so your middle finger is at the sixth fret and your other two fingers are at the seventh fret. This is an Aadd9. Finally, go up two more frets so your fingers are at the eighth and ninth frets. Now you have a Badd4. Pretty cool, eh? Actually, you may hear some string noise when you slide that you're not too happy about. Just live with it for the time being. Try to keep your index finger relaxed and close to the strings throughout the progression. Continue strumming and slide back down to E at the first and second frets. Play through the changes a few more times so that you get used to making shifts up and down the neck.

Now it's time to pay attention to your left thumb. Your thumbprint should only be about halfway up the back of the guitar's neck, and your thumb should be pointing up. This is important. To get a sense of the best shape for your hand to take, touch the thumbprint part of your thumb with the tip of your left-hand middle finger. Now separate your thumb and fingertip an inch or less and imagine the guitar neck between your thumb and fingertip. As you do this, you will have probably bent your wrist a little, too, so that the palm of your hand faces your chest. This is pretty close to the perfect barre chord position.

Now finish up the job, with Example 2:

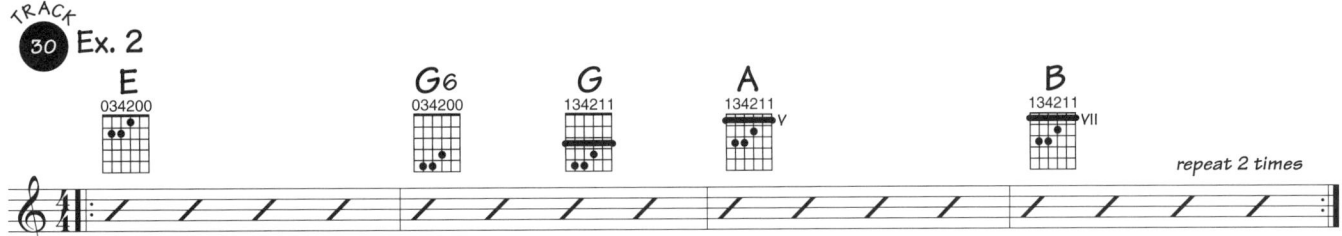

Example 2 is the same as Example 1 except that this time, after you've strummed the G6 chord twice, you lay your index finger across all six strings and strum two more times. Don't stop strumming to put your index finger down. Using a metronome can help keep your right hand going. Still strumming, slide this new chord up two more frets, so your index finger is at the fifth fret. Strum four times, then slide two more frets, so your index finger is at the seventh fret. Don't stop strumming when you make the chord changes; you want to keep a nice rhythm going. Play through this progression a few times. When you barre at the third fret, the G6 chord becomes a G chord; when you barre at the fifth fret, the Aadd9 becomes an A chord; and when you barre at the seventh fret, the Badd4 becomes a B.

Try the progression again, this time leaving out the G6 step and going directly from the E to the G chord with the barre at the third fret.

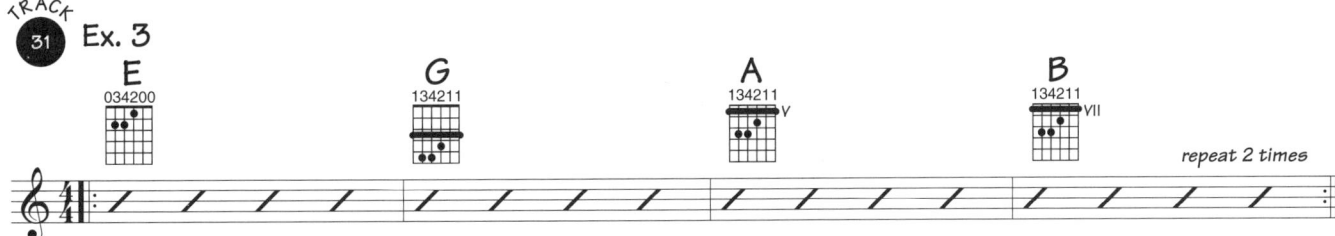

This is a more conventional sound, but it loses a little of the drama of Example 2.

The issue here isn't strength, although it does takes some. It's more important to hold a position in which your left hand can work efficiently. Keeping your wrist bent and your thumb low and parallel to your other fingers is the key. Muted or buzzing strings can be cured with small shifts of hand or finger position. You can isolate which strings and fingers are causing problems, but don't do it while you're working on the chord changes.

Here's a chart that shows the names of the chords you create by using this E-chord shape and barring different frets up the neck all the way to the tenth fret. On most non-cutaway acoustic guitars, full barre chords above the tenth fret are difficult.

E-Shape Barre Chords

I	II	III	IV	V	VI	VII	VIII	IX	X
F	F#/Gb	G	G#/Ab	A	A#/Bb	B	C	C#/Db	D

Thousands of songs, plain and fancy, use barre chords. Two chestnuts that really sound good when played with barre chords are Otis Redding's "Dock of the Bay" and the folk/country classic "Abilene." Use this blues progression in F to play some of your favorite blues tunes:

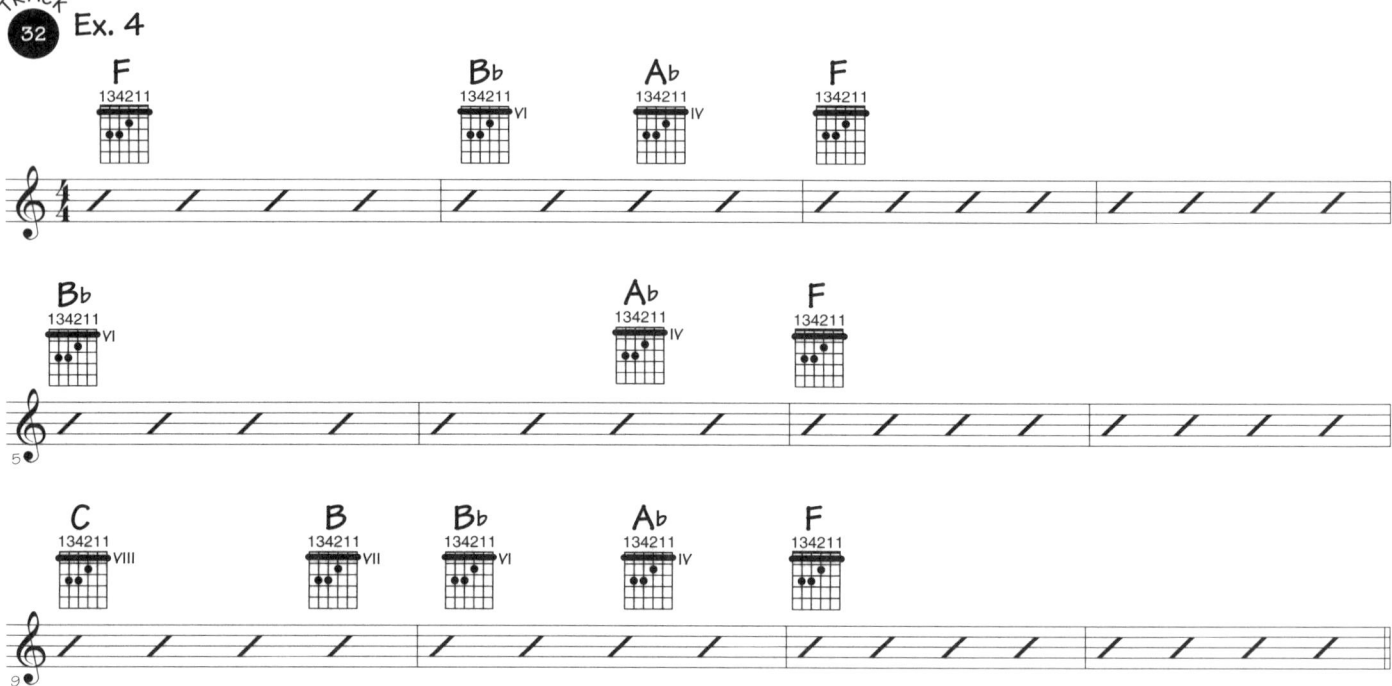

Here's another song that will allow you to practice your newly learned barre chords. I start the old folk classic "Down in the Valley" in the key of E and then modulate up a half step to F.

MOVING ON

Down in the Valley
Traditional, arranged by John Gribble

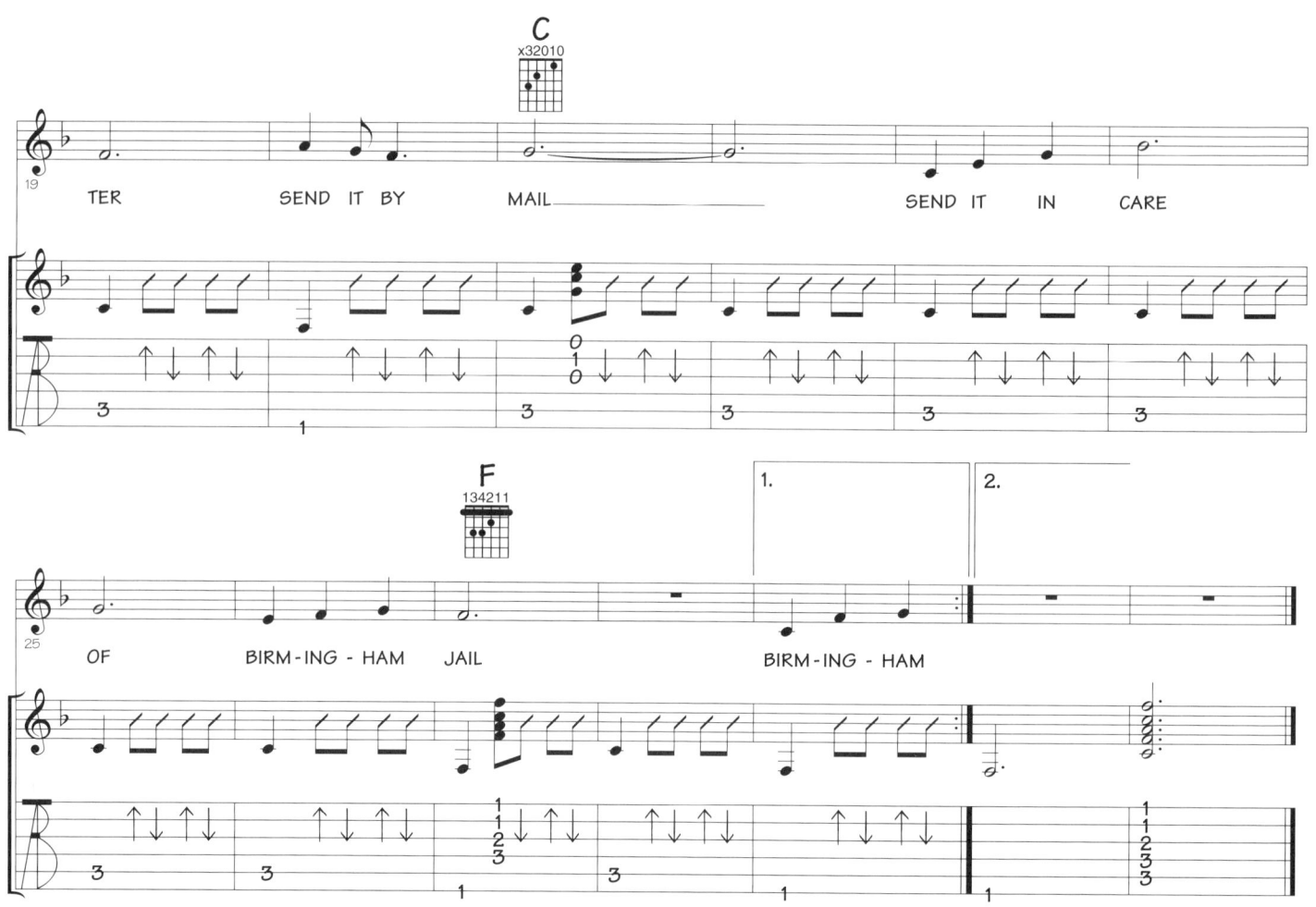

1. DOWN IN THE VALLEY, VALLEY SO LOW
   LATE IN THE EVENING HEAR THE WINDS BLOW
   HEAR THE WIND BLOW LOVE HEAR THE WIND BLOW
   LATE IN THE EVENING HEAR THE WIND BLOW

2. IF YOU DON'T LOVE ME LOVE WHOM YOU PLEASE
   THROW YOUR ARMS 'ROUND ME GIVE MY HEART EASE
   GIVE MY HEART EASE LOVE GIVE MY HEART EASE
   THROW YOUR ARMS 'ROUND ME GIVE MY HEART EASE

3. WRITE ME A LETTER SEND IT BY MAIL
   SEND IT IN CARE OF BIRMINGHAM JAIL
   BIRMINGHAM JAIL LOVE BIRMINGHAM JAIL
   SEND IT IN CARE OF BIRMINGHAM JAIL

MOVING ON

Moving Bass Lines
Happy Traum

You are probably familiar with the bass runs that most guitarists use to connect the chords of a folk or country song. These three or four bass notes move up and down the diatonic scale, usually starting on the root of one chord and ending up on the root of the next. They are very useful in that they add interest to a song and often provide a nice harmony to the sung melody line. (For a few examples, see my lesson "Folk Song Accompaniment.")

Another easy way to provide interest to a song accompaniment is to add a moving bass line under the melody. This effective device is not just a bridge between chords. A continuous bass line becomes an integral part of the song, providing a sense of movement and grace in the melody. You can use a moving bass for a measure or two, or it can flow through much of the song.

I'm sure you know the beautiful ballad "The Water Is Wide." It's been sung and recorded by nearly every folksinger and quite a few pop artists as well. Two of my favorite versions in recent years are by Rory Block (on *Best Blues and Originals,* Rounder) and James Taylor (on *New Moon Shine,* Columbia). Each time "The Water Is Wide" is done it sounds a little different, which is probably the mark of a great song. Like many such ballads, it can be harmonized many different ways. The version on page 38

is the way I like to do it.

The right hand picks basic arpeggios: Your thumb plays the bass notes on the sixth, fifth, and fourth strings; and your index, middle, and ring fingers pick the third, second, and first strings, respectively. You can vary the arpeggio pattern as you like, as long as the rhythm stays steady and even. Be sure the bass notes ring out with a strong, clear tone.

These moving lines seem to fall most easily in the key of C. Hold the C chord, keeping your first finger down on the C note (second string, first fret) while you move the bass notes with your second and third fingers. Since you are only playing the arpeggio on the top three strings, you don't have to worry about the fourth string.

Introduction — TRACK 34

A continuous bass line provides a sense of movement and grace in the melody.

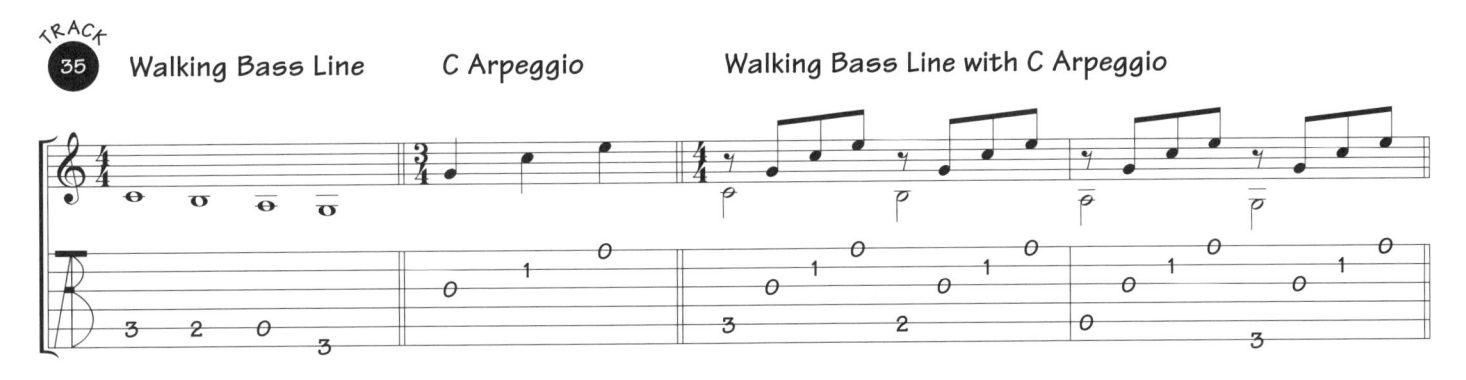

TRACK 35 — Walking Bass Line — C Arpeggio — Walking Bass Line with C Arpeggio

Similarly, when you go to the G chord, simply hold the high G while you move the bass notes on the lower strings. It should be very clear if you follow the tab and music. You'll see that the descending line starts on the F, or seventh of the chord (fourth string, third fret), and moves down the scale, ending conveniently on the root (C) of the C chord. In the third line of the song ("Build me a boat . . ."), your bass line follows a continuous movement from F (on beat 3 of measure 9) to C to low G (sixth string, third fret). The phrase ends by skipping F and finishing on the open A of the A minor chord.

Track 36 — Walking Bass Line with G Arpeggio

The Water Is Wide

Traditional, arranged by Happy Traum

Track 37 — Capo IV
Intro / Verse

C — 1. THE WAT-ER IS WIDE
F — I CAN'T CROSS O-
G — VER
C — AND NEITH-ER HAVE
D9 — I WINGS TO FLY
G
C — BUILD ME A BOAT
Am — THAT WILL CAR-RY TWO
F — AND BOTH SHALL ROW

MOVING ON

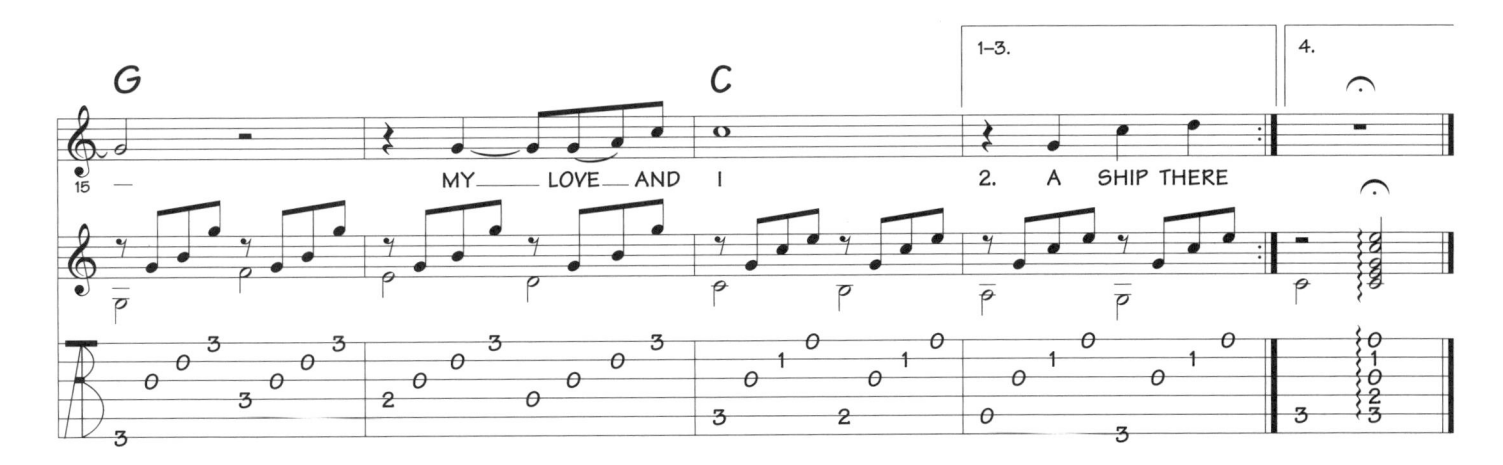

1. THE WATER IS WIDE, I CAN'T CROSS OVER
   AND NEITHER HAVE I WINGS TO FLY
   BUILD ME A BOAT THAT WILL CARRY TWO
   AND BOTH SHALL ROW, MY LOVE AND I

2. A SHIP THERE IS, AND SHE SAILS THE SEAS
   SHE'S LADEN DEEP AS DEEP CAN BE
   BUT NOT SO DEEP AS THE LOVE I'M IN
   AND I KNOW NOT IF I SINK OR SWIM

3. I LEANED MY BACK AGAINST A YOUNG OAK
   THINKING HE WERE A TRUSTY TREE
   BUT FIRST HE BENT AND THEN HE BROKE
   THUS DID MY LOVE PROVE FALSE TO ME

4. OH, LOVE IS HANDSOME AND LOVE IS KIND
   GAY AS A JEWEL WHEN FIRST IT'S NEW
   BUT LOVE GROWS OLD AND WAXES COLD
   AND FADES AWAY LIKE THE MORNING DEW

You can try transposing to other keys, and by experimenting you'll get the feel of what the harmonic possibilities are. Once you've got this song under your belt, try to come up with others in which you can use moving bass lines. For instance, Jerry Jeff Walker's "Mr. Bojangles" on page 40 uses this device very effectively. It's usually played in C, and it's in 3/4 or waltz time. The first four measures are sung over the C chord, then you go to F (use a barred version of the chord for the low F note) and G or G7. Try playing each bass note of the descending line (C B A G F) followed by two strums across the top three strings, as shown below.

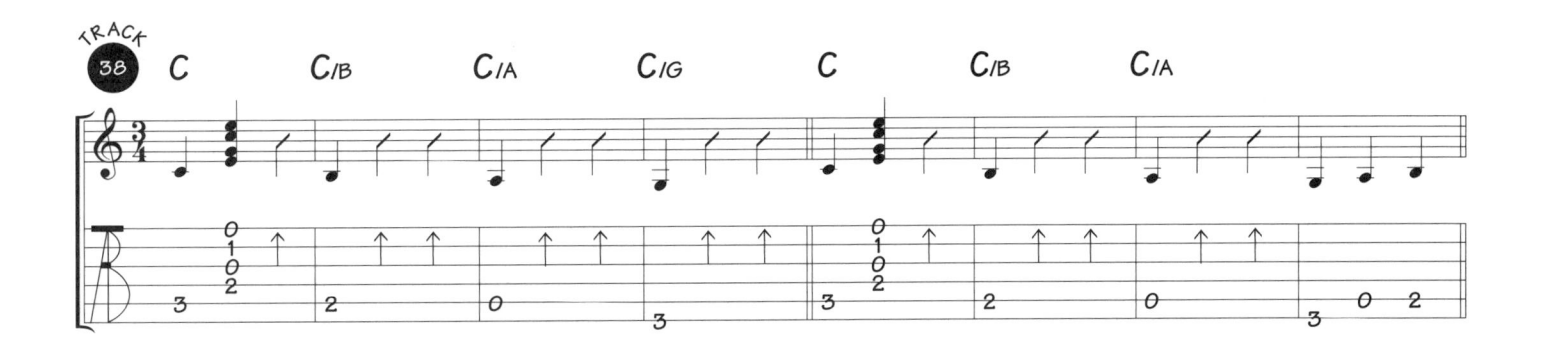

Mr. Bojangles

Words and music by Jerry Jeff Walker

1. I KNEW A MAN BOJANGLES AND HE DANCED FOR YOU
   IN WORN OUT SHOES
   WITH SILVER HAIR A RAGGED SHIRT AND BAGGY PANTS
   DID THE OLD SOFT SHOE
   HE JUMPED SO HIGH, JUMPED SO HIGH
   AND HE LIGHTLY TOUCHED DOWN

       MISTER BOJANGLES
       MISTER BOJANGLES
       MISTER BOJANGLES
       DANCE

2. I MET HIM IN A CELL IN NEW ORLEANS
   I WAS DOWN AND OUT
   HE LOOKED TO BE THE EYES OF AGE
   AS HE SPOKE RIGHT OUT
   HE TALKED OF LIFE, HE TALKED OF LIFE
   HE LAUGHED, SLAPPED HIS LEG A STEP

       CHORUS

3. HE SAID HIS NAME BOJANGLES THEN HE DANCED A LICK
   ACROSS THE CELL
   HE GRABBED A CHAIR LIKE FRED ASTAIRE THEN JUMPED UP HIGH
   HE CLICKED HIS HEELS
   HE LET GO A LAUGH, HE LET GO A LAUGH
   SHOOK BACK HIS CLOTHES ALL AROUND

       CHORUS

4. HE DANCED FOR THOSE AT MINSTREL SHOWS AND COUNTY FAIRS
   THROUGHOUT THE SOUTH
   HE SPOKE WITH TEARS OF 15 YEARS HOW HIS DOG AND HE
   TRAVELED ABOUT
   HIS DOG UP AND DIED, UP AND DIED
   AFTER 20 YEARS HE STILL GRIEVED

       CHORUS

5. HE SAID "I DANCE NOW AT EVERY CHANCE IN HONKY-TONKS
   FOR DRINKS AND TIPS
   BUT MOST OF THE TIME I SPEND BEHIND THESE COUNTY BARS"
   HE SAID "I DRINKS A BIT"
   HE SHOOK HIS HEAD AND AS HE SHOOK HIS HEAD
   I HEARD SOMEONE ASK PLEASE

       CHORUS

Using a Capo

David Hamburger

A capo is designed to raise all six strings of the guitar an equal amount. For example, putting the capo on at the second fret is like tuning every string up one whole step: E becomes F♯, A becomes B, and so on, giving you F♯ B E A C♯ F♯. Now, if you've ever accidentally tuned your low string to the wrong pitch and tuned the rest of the guitar to that, you know that it doesn't matter what pitch the guitar's strings are at, as long as they're all in tune with each other. You can still make all the same chords, they just might not be in tune with everyone else around you. So, if you put the capo at the second fret, you can still form all the same chords. However—and this is an important however—the same chord shapes will now give you, in terms of absolute pitch, all different chords.

ACCOMMODATING YOUR VOICE

The most basic and important use of the capo is to change the key of a song to suit your voice. Let's say you know a song in the key of G with the chords G, C, and D. You've got a great arrangement in G, and you can play the chords in your sleep while you sing the song. The only problem is, G is kind of low for your voice. If you put the capo at the second fret, you can continue to play the same arrangement with all the same fingerings, but it will come out in a higher key. To know what chords you're playing, you'll have to raise the name of each chord by the same amount that you've capoed up the neck. So, if you've capoed up two frets or a whole step, your G-shaped chord is now sounding like an A chord, your C-shaped chord is now yielding a D, and your D-shaped chord is sounding like an E. Play the top line of Example 1 while someone else plays the bottom line, which is the same chord progression played without a capo using open A, D, and E chords.

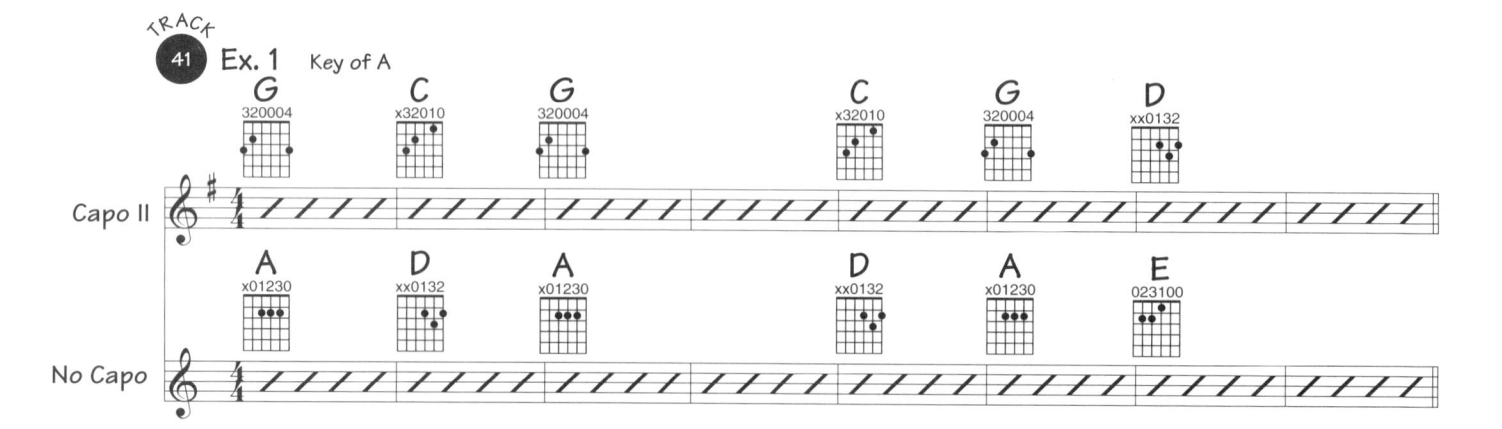

The capo does more than just let you transpose keys.

If you're trying to raise the key of a tune in E for your voice, you'll be in the key of F if you capo at the first fret and in F♯ at the second fret. Capoing three frets will put you in the key of G, at which point you could remove the capo in favor of using the familiar first-position G, C, and D chords. If you want to play in G♯ (maybe you like listening to fiddle players grumble), you could keep playing E shapes but capo on the fourth fret, or you could use open-G shapes and capo at the first fret as shown in Example 2.

TRACK 42 Ex. 2 Key of G#

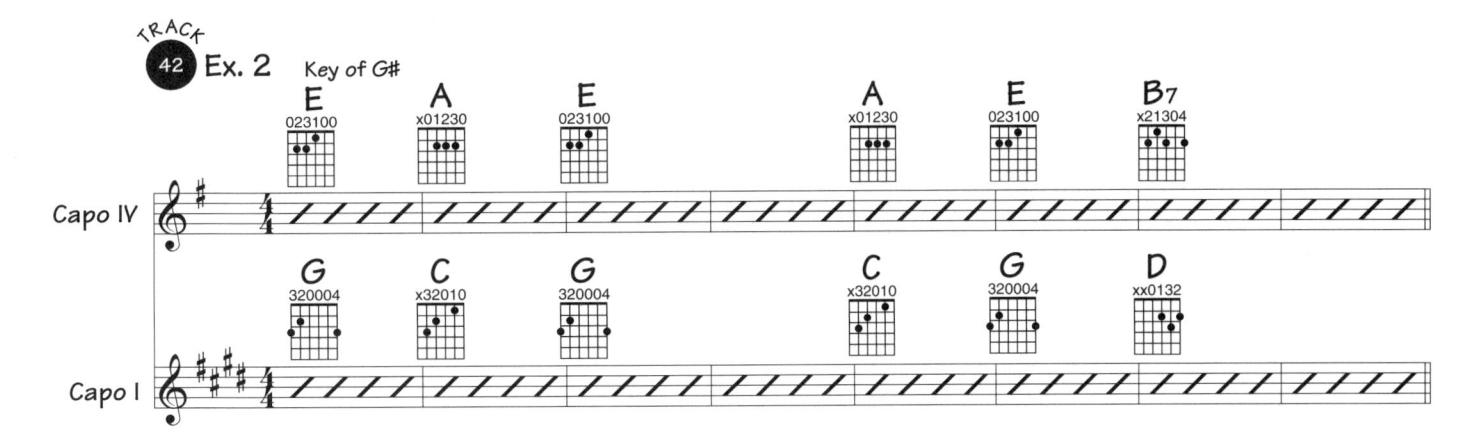

[Musical notation: Capo IV line shows chords E, A, E, A, E, B7. Capo I line shows chords G, C, G, C, G, D.]

Here's a chart that shows what chords you get with the five basic open chord shapes as you place the capo on frets one through seven.

Chord Shapes Capoed up the Neck

No capo	Capo I	II	III	IV	V	VI	VII
C	C#/Db	D	D#/Eb	E	F	F#/Gb	G
A	A#/Bb	B	C	C#/Db	D	D#/Eb	E
G	G#/Ab	A	A#/Bb	B	C	C#/Db	D
E	F	F#/Gb	G	G#/Ab	A	A#/Bb	B
D	D#/Eb	E	F	F#/Gb	G	G#/Ab	A

VARYING CHORD VOICINGS

As you may be realizing, the capo does more than just let you transpose keys. It also lets you begin to make more creative choices about what "key shapes" to use. Each of the standard major open-position keys on the guitar—G, C, E, A, and D—has distinctive qualities and possibilities. To think about our last example again, playing uncapoed in G has a big open sound, which is popular in country and bluegrass music. The chord voicings in the key of E often lend things a more bluesy quality, particularly because the easiest V chord to grab in the key of E is an open B7 chord, which has been used in countless blues guitar arrangements. So by capoing at the third fret and using E chord shapes to play in the key of G, it almost doesn't matter how you pick or strum the song; the chord shapes you've chosen are going to have a substantial impact on the overall effect you create. Keeping this in mind, you can keep a song in the same key while using the capo to allow a certain quality to come through.

Bob Dylan's "Don't Think Twice, It's Alright" is an excellent example of this approach. For years I wondered why Bob made it all the way through this song in the key of E without ever hitting a big fat low E string. For that matter, I wondered why a folkie in 1962 was using things like C#7 barre chords and why I didn't hear the strings squeak as he moved those barre chords around. Well, it turns out he recorded the tune capoed at the fourth fret so he could get that Mississippi John Hurt sort of sound by using the shapes from the key of C. Capo a C chord up to the fourth fret and it is an E chord, even though in guitaristic terms it still *sounds* like a C chord.

LOWERING THE KEY

You can also use a capo to lower the key. I know that sounds weird, but it's true. Let's return to our I–IV–V song in G (i.e., it uses the chords G, C, and D). Suppose G is too high a key for your voice, but F would be perfect. Well, we all know that playing acoustic guitar in the key of F is about as much fun as being a low-flying pigeon at an Ozzy Osbourne show, so what's the alternative? Try capoing at the third fret and using the chord shapes of the key of D as shown in Example 3. Your D will sound like an F, your G will sound like a B♭, and your A will sound like a C. There you go: F, B♭, and C are the I, IV, and V in the key of F. And best of all, no gnarly barre chords to wrestle with.

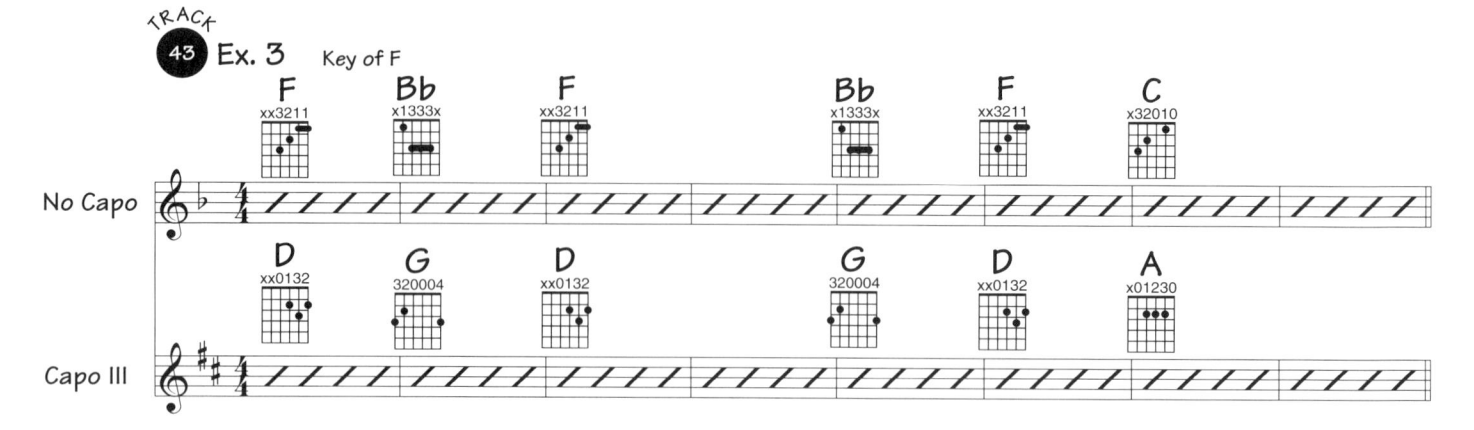

TRACK 43 Ex. 3   Key of F

B♭ is another key that's hard to play in. If you've written a song in C that's just a bit too high for you, see if you can rework it using G shapes and a capo on the third fret. Your G becomes the B♭, your C becomes the E♭, and your D becomes the F—giving you B♭, E♭, and F, or the I, IV, and V in the key of B♭.

CREATING SECOND GUITAR PARTS

Aside from the practicalities of working around the range of your voice and the idiosyncracies of the fretboard, one of the most common uses of the capo is to create second guitar parts, for either playing in a duo or overdubbing on a recording. For this kind of approach, you may very well want to capo higher. Matching a part played at the fifth or seventh fret with an open-position part can make for one great big sparkling guitar sound or create the impression of a 12-string guitar. Take a look at Example 4:

TRACK 44 Ex. 4   Key of G

Tape yourself or get a friend to play the first guitar part in open G, fingerpicked, and see what it sounds like combined with the second part, played with D shapes capoed at the fifth fret.

For a recorded example of the shimmer you can create by capoing higher up the neck, give a listen to George Harrison on the Beatles' "Here Comes the Sun," which uses D shapes capoed at the seventh fret.

OPEN TUNINGS

Open tunings are another place where the capo can be quite useful. All of the great ringing-string sounds and interesting voicings made possible in open tunings completely disappear once you have to start using barre chords. So capos and open tunings really go hand in hand. The capo will let you change keys to suit your voice and will let you use the same tuning for a couple of songs in a row without wearing out the sound of one particular key. In addition, the capo lets you use the same tuning to play bottleneck or slide guitar in more than one key. The way the capo pulls the strings down to the fretboard makes it harder to get a good slide sound than when uncapoed, but slide players from Robert Johnson to Ry Cooder have made use of the capo to raise open-D tuning up to E or F and open G up to A, B♭, or B. Example 5 shows how you can use open D (D A D F♯ A D) to play in the key of F by capoing at the third fret.

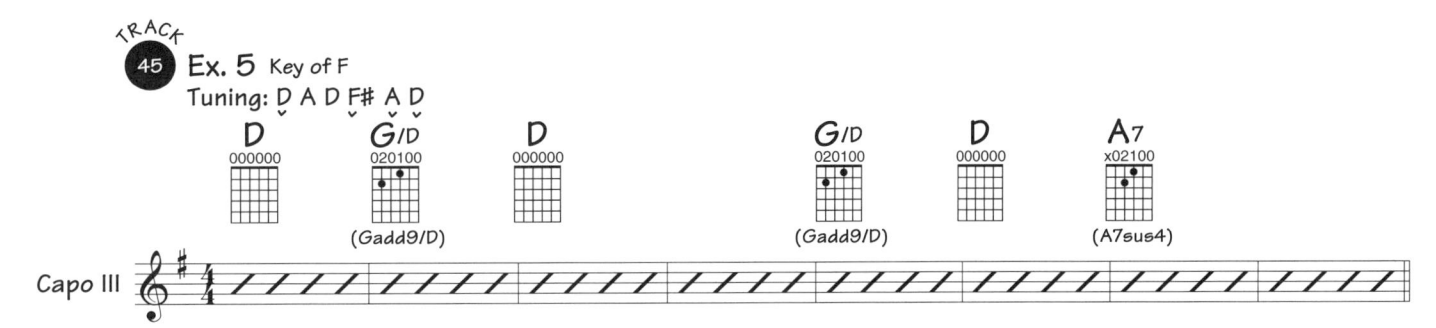

TRACK 45 Ex. 5 Key of F
Tuning: D A D F♯ A D

Capo III

Capoed open tunings also make great second guitar parts. In Example 6 on page 46, open-position C shapes sound in contrast to a complementary part in open-G tuning (D G D G B D) capoed at the fifth fret.

LEARNING OFF RECORDS

Now that we've looked at the capo from both a practical and a creative point of view, I should point out one more use: investigative tool. As you're trying to figure out guitar parts off of recordings, bear in mind that someone could be using one of the approaches we've talked about here to wax their immortal tracks. Listen for the sound of open strings, and try to identify which chord shapes you're hearing based on your own familiarity with the sound of the five basic shapes—G, C, D, A, and E. Then, if you can't find those sounds on your own guitar in the open position, try to figure out what key the song is in and begin trying various capo positions up the neck.

ACOUSTIC GUITAR ACCOMPANIMENT BASICS

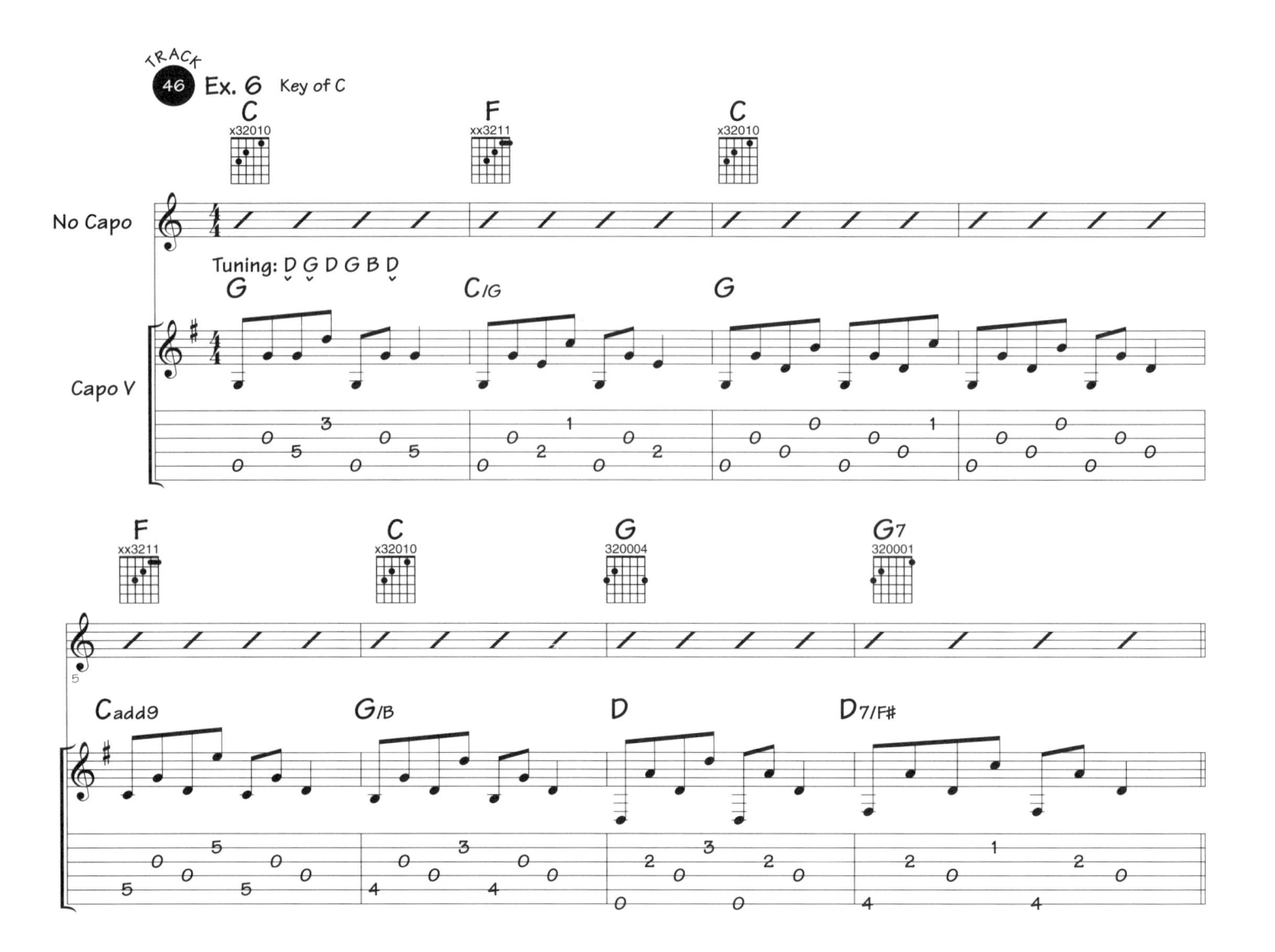

TRACK 46 Ex. 6 Key of C

MOVING ON

Rock Rhythm
David Hamburger

The big myth about playing blues and rock rhythm guitar is that you have to play barre chords. It's true that barre chords sound a whole lot different than strummy, open-position "cowboy chords," but players (even electric players) rarely hold down all six strings of a barre chord. Most rely on the classic power chord: just the bottom two strings.

Another thing to keep in mind is that there's more to rhythm guitar than just chonking away on a complete chord. The lower wound strings are often beefy enough to carry through as single-note riffs. Double-stops—when you play two notes together—work well if you're playing with another guitar player or a bass player. And triads—three-note voicings—can be grabbed with three individual fingers and, with sufficient left-hand damping, moved around the neck to create convincing parts.

Finally, you can work off of the open strings, especially the low E and A, and use a capo to do the rest. Open strings rule on the acoustic guitar; they're your chief tool in generating sustain. And sustain is the key. Unlike an electric guitarist, you don't have a solid-body instrument or a chiming, ringing amplifier to help you out, so open strings help to pick up the slack. There are really only two basic power/barre chord shapes to move around the neck, A and E, and you can make the most of them by using a capo at various positions.

Let's begin by demystifying those barre chords. Here are the two classic barre chord shapes played at the third fret to give you a G chord and a C chord:

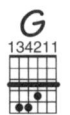

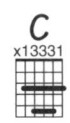

There's more to rhythm guitar than just chonking away on a complete chord.

Introduction — TRACK 47

Notice the shapes of the chords. If you stare at them long enough, it should become clear that the first chord is basically an E chord moved up to the third fret, with your index-finger barre acting as a capo would to raise the rest of the strings. And the second chord is essentially an open-position A chord moved up to the third fret in the same way.

Don't worry if you can't get these chords to sound clean right now. We'll be starting out with the abbreviated power-chord versions of these voicings:

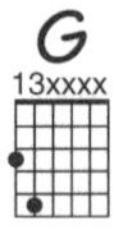

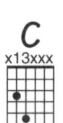

Play lazy: let the fleshy underside of your fingers rest on the upper strings to mute them as you strum down on the bottom two strings.

TRACK 48 Swing ($\sqcap = \overset{3}{\sqcap}$)

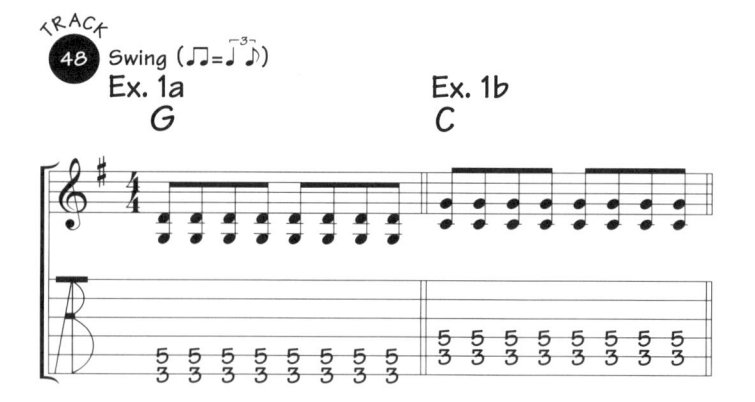

Ex. 1a — G

Ex. 1b — C

Got all that? Now we're going to drop in the capo to allow us to do more with these sounds than just crank out the root and the fifth (although in some cases, that's exactly what the situation calls for). By placing a capo at the third fret, we can now get this same voicing with just one finger. Plus, we get an open string on the bottom. This lets us play the classic vamp in Example 2a without wrenching our tendons. Although the notation now says you're playing an E chord, the capo raises the actual pitch to G (this is the standard way to notate a capoed part). Try playing this with and without palm muting. Palm muting is when you rest the soft outer side of your picking hand just where the strings meet the bridge to create a sound that doesn't ring out so much. Example 2b shows another common variation on this basic rhythm riff.

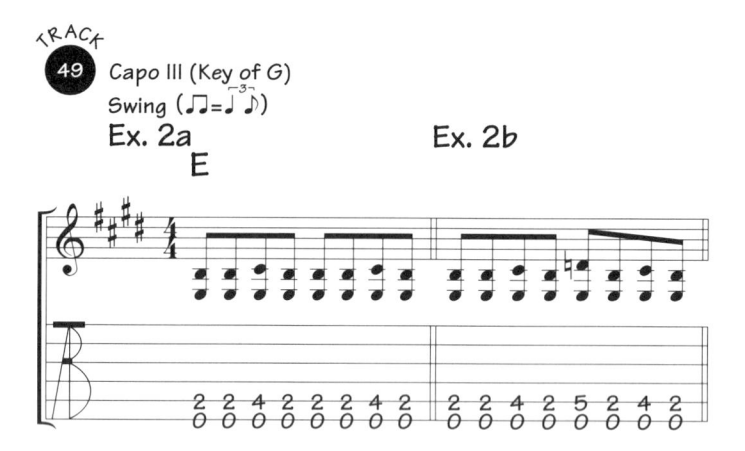

TRACK 49 Capo III (Key of G)
Swing ($\sqcap = \overset{3}{\sqcap}$)

Ex. 2a — E

Ex. 2b

Simply move either of these phrases over one string to play them as an A chord (which actually sounds as a C, with the capo); here's one more possible variation on this approach.

TRACK 50 Swing ($\sqcap = \overset{3}{\sqcap}$)

Ex. 3 — A

Let's try putting this together into a 12-bar blues. Example 4 is a blues in E that combines the various riffs we've learned so far. Since there is no open bass string for the V chord (B), just play the basic eighth-note downstroke strum for bars 9 and 12.

Example 5a comes from a different school of thought. Buddy Guy often played backup parts like this with Junior Wells in the 1960s; it comes from a time when guitarists lacking a bass player would comp for one another by imitating bass lines. By capoing at the third fret again, we can use an open string for the lowest note and move up the fretboard to grab the remainder of the line on the heftier fourth and fifth strings, as in Example 5b.

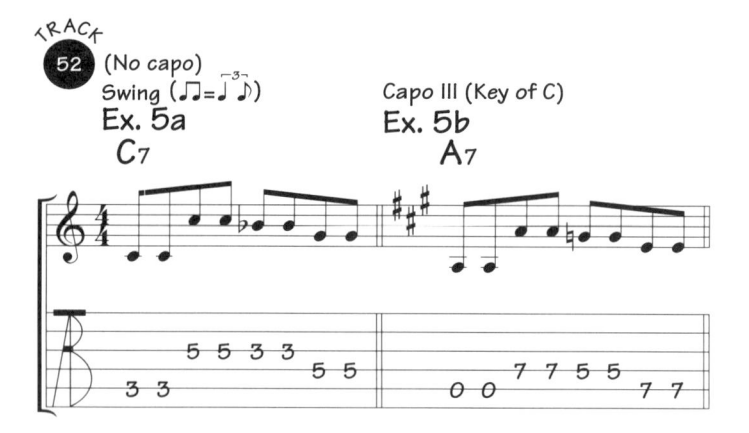

This position is good for working out a few chord-based licks as well. In Example 6a, make a partial barre with your ring finger across the seventh fret (counting the fret after the capo as one). Next, make another partial barre with your index finger at the fifth fret and hammer on from the minor to the major third (C♮ to C♯) with your second finger on the third string. This classic blues figure has been used countless times. Example 6b shows a way to combine it with an open string–based single-note rhythm riff that lies nicely on the acoustic guitar.

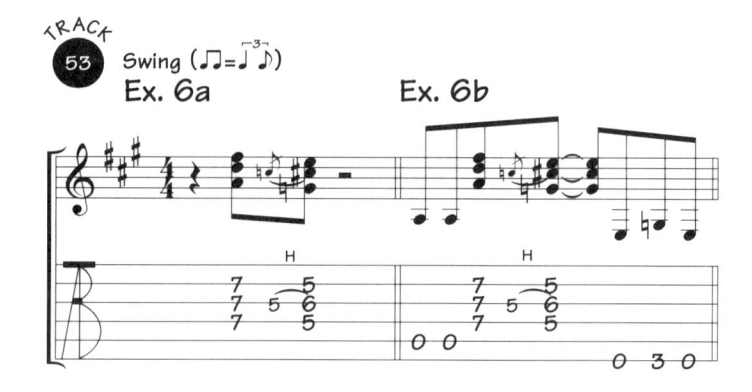

You may recognize the chord in Example 7 as most of an open-position C7 chord moved up the neck. As with the power chords above, let the soft undersides of your fretting fingers mute the unwanted strings. Example 7 combines this abbreviated three-note chord voicing with a single-note bass riff.

MOVING ON

Example 8 is a 12-bar blues in A. Notice that one of our earlier double-stop riffs works well over the V chord in measure 9, while the single-note idea is adapted to the same chord in measure 12.

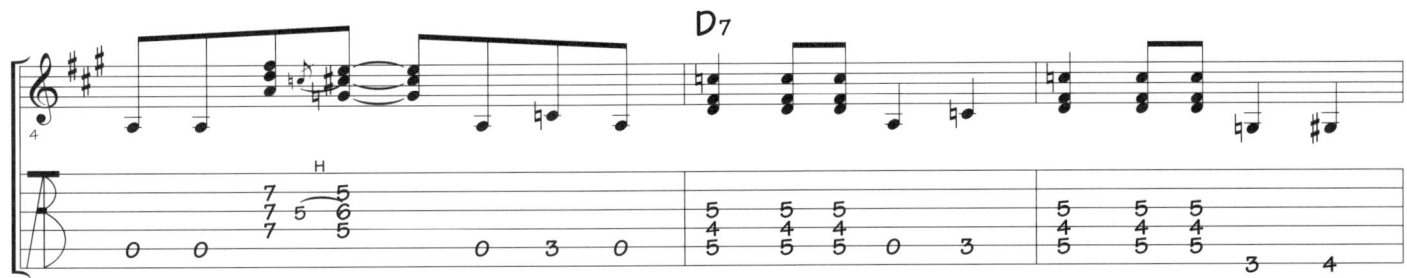

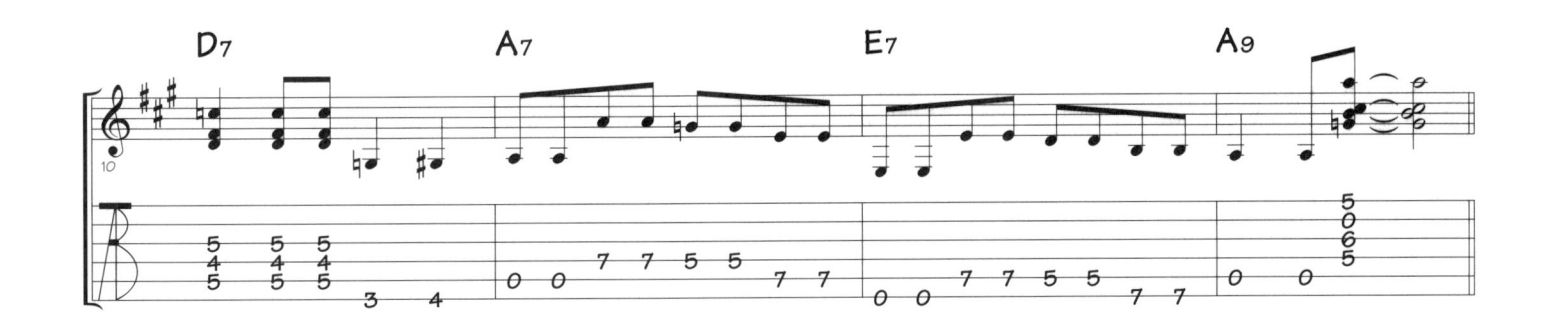

TRACK 55 Swing ($\sqcap = \sqcap^3$)

Ex. 8

Finally, here's an eight-bar blues using a lot of the ideas we've explored. Now you're ready for some serious unamplified grooving.

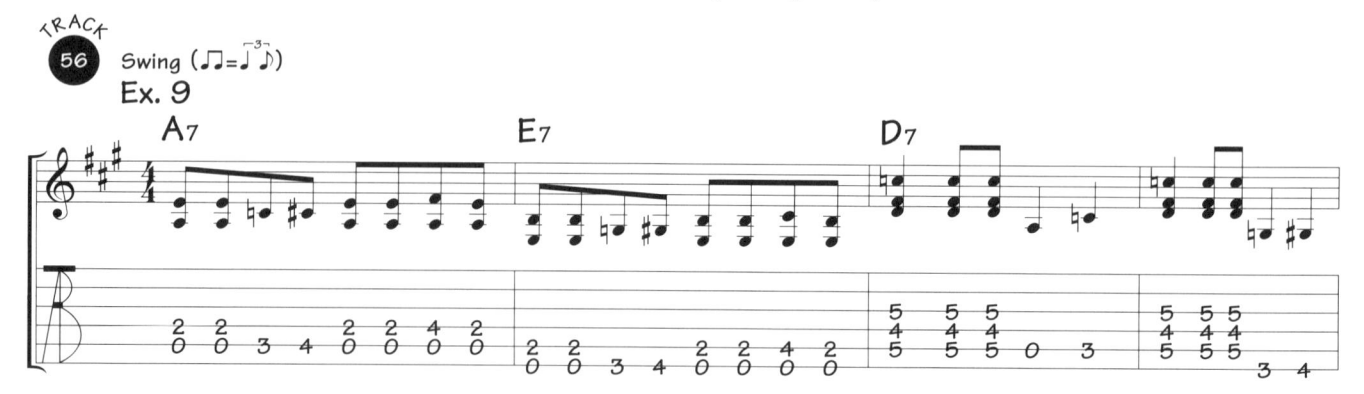

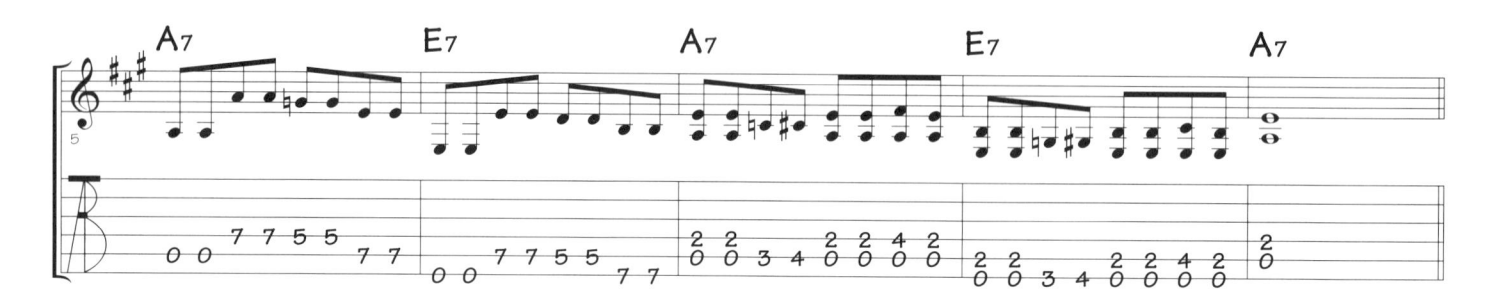

MOVING ON

Chord Embellishment
Dylan Schorer

My first attempt at playing guitar involved learning simple open chords. Once I had a few major chords conquered, I was shown my first minor chord. I remember how dark and ominous that Em chord sounded after a week of strumming A, E, C, and D chords. Then somebody showed me how to play power chords on the electric guitar, which kept me busy for a while. Eventually power chords started to sound powerless, and I sought out as many new chords as I could find. I was a chord junkie. I didn't know the names of many of the chords I learned, but I knew the mood and emotion that each one invoked in me.

Eventually, I learned the names of most of the chords I had been writing down in a notebook: major sevens sounded mellow and jazzy; nines sounded bluesy; sixes had a Hawaiian flair; diminished chords sounded ragtimey (or like background music in a cheap melodrama if you worked a diminished-seven chord up the neck, fret by fret); I recognized augmented chords as the arpeggiated opening chords to countless '50s rock ballads. I also loved the sound of add-nine, minor-add-nine, suspended-second, and minor-nine chords. It was obvious that many of my favorite chords had a nine or a two in their name. I didn't know what that meant, but I knew that I liked the sound. Play the following chords and see what emotions they invoke in you.

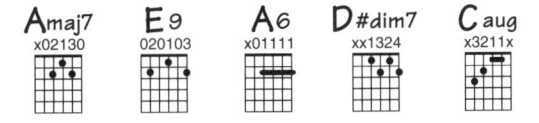

Amaj7 E9 A6 D#dim7 Caug
x02130 020103 x01111 xx1324 x3211x

Before long, I knew plenty of chords, but no songs. When I did learn a few tunes, I was never content to play a song exactly like everyone else; I wanted it to sound like the original, but with my own ideas thrown in. I didn't know much about licks or fills at the time, so I'd simply alter a few of the chords here and there. For instance, I might change a C chord to a Cmaj7 or an Am to an Am7 or Amadd9. By making these subtle changes, I was able to play my own unique version of a song and still have it be easily recognized. Often the chords that I substituted were even easier to play than the original chords. Actually, I wasn't technically *substituting* a chord, but rather *embellishing* the original chord; if the letter name of the chords remains the same (C to Cmaj7, for example), it is a chord embellishment.

To embellish a tune with alternate chord voicings, you need to know what your options are:

Chord Type	Can Be Replaced with
Major	Major 7, major 9, 6, add 9, suspended 2
Minor	Minor 7, minor 9, minor add 9, suspended 2
Seven	9, 11, 13, 7♯9, 7 suspended 4

These chord names may sound intimidating, but the fingerings are often very easy.

One or two well-placed embellishments can make an arrangement entirely your own.

Introduction — TRACK 57

To get an idea of how chord embellishments can breathe new life into a progression, try fingerpicking the following basic C-to-Am progression:

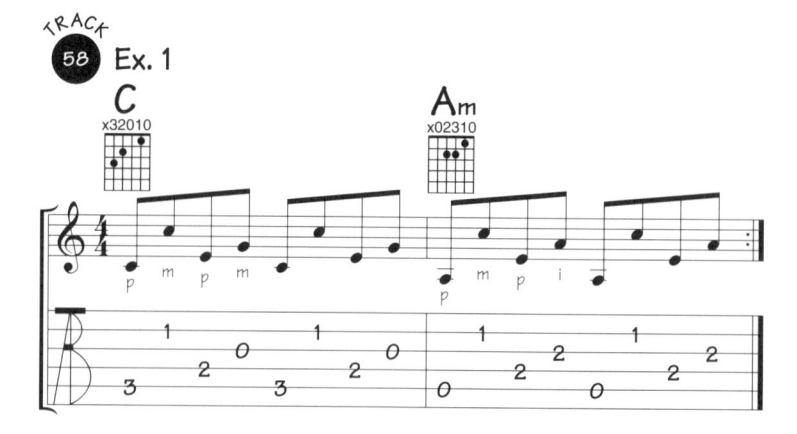

TRACK 58 Ex. 1

Now try the following embellishment, in which the C has been changed to a Cmaj7, and the Am has been changed to an Am7:

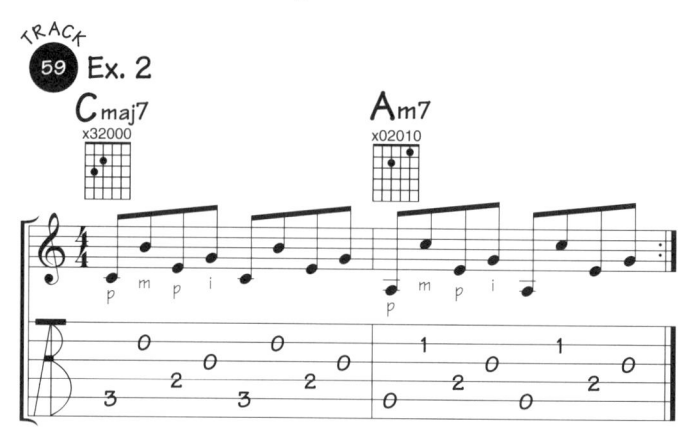

TRACK 59 Ex. 2

Now try this alternative, in which the C has been replaced with a Cadd9 and the Am has been replaced with an Amadd9. Your left hand needs to jump up to the fifth fret to play the Amadd9 chord, but the open string on the last beat of the Cadd9 chord and the first beat of the Amadd9 gives you time to make the switch. Notice in this second variation that the fingerpicking pattern has been altered slightly.

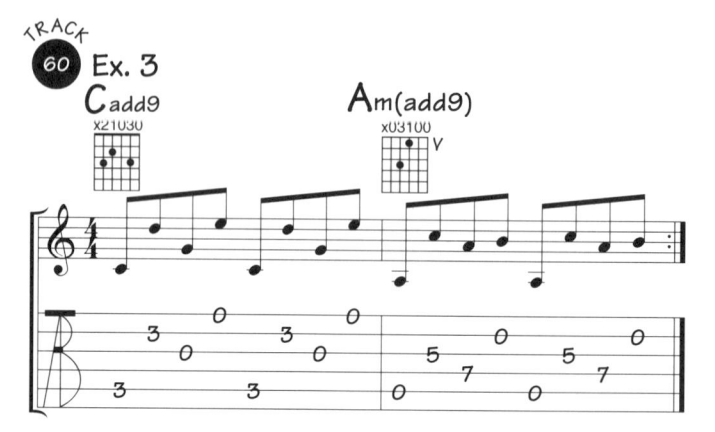

TRACK 60 Ex. 3

Add-nine, minor-add-nine, and suspended-second chords are some of the easiest chords to use because they don't alter the mood of a piece drastically but simply add a little dissonance. Remember that add-nine chords can replace major chords, and minor-add-nine chords can replace minor chords. Suspended-second chords are very similar to add-nine chords (the two is the same note as the nine), except that suspended-second chords do not contain a third—the note that identifies a chord as major or minor. Because of this, suspended-second chords can replace either major or minor chords and can be used interchangeably with add-nine and minor-add-nine chords. Here are some common fingerings for seven-chord embellishments:

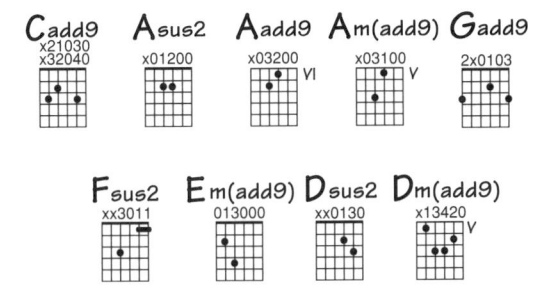

Cadd9 (x21030 / x32040) Asus2 (x01200) Aadd9 (x03200) Am(add9) (x03100) VI V Gadd9 (2x0103)

Fsus2 (xx3011) Em(add9) (013000) Dsus2 (xx0130) Dm(add9) (x13420) V

Major-seven, minor-seven, major-nine, minor-nine, six, minor-six, and minor-11 chords also make nice substitutions, but they alter the mood of the piece more than add-nine chords do. Experiment and let your ears tell you whether a particular embellishment is right for a tune. Here are some more chord fingerings to play around with:

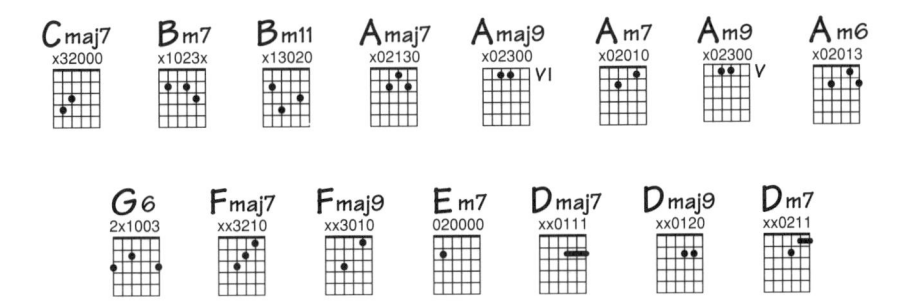

Cmaj7 (x32000) Bm7 (x1023x) Bm11 (x13020) Amaj7 (x02130) Amaj9 (x02300) VI Am7 (x02010) Am9 (x02300) V Am6 (x02013)

G6 (2x1003) Fmaj7 (xx3210) Fmaj9 (xx3010) Em7 (020000) Dmaj7 (xx0111) Dmaj9 (xx0120) Dm7 (xx0211)

Seven chords can be embellished with nine, 11, 13, seven-suspended-four, add-nine, and suspended-second chords. Also note that the V chord in each key can be played as a seven chord and embellished as such. Here are some fingerings for seven-chord embellishments:

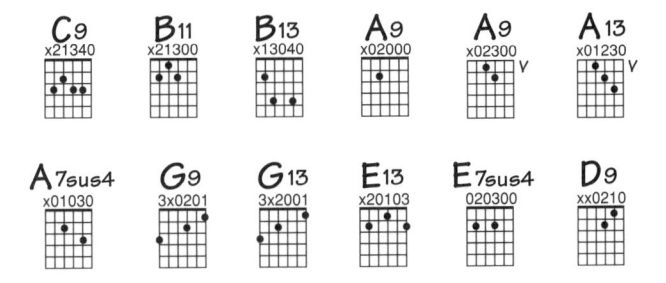

C9 (x21340) B11 (x21300) B13 (x13040) A9 (x02000) A9 (x02300) V A13 (x01230) V

A7sus4 (x01030) G9 (3x0201) G13 (3x2001) E13 (x20103) E7sus4 (020300) D9 (xx0210)

Try applying these principles of chord embellishment to the Irish air "Star of the County Down" below. First play through the original chords, either fingerpicking or lightly strumming through the progression. Then try putting in a few embellishments of your choice—maybe an Am(add9) in place of the Am, or an Fmaj7 in place of the F. See what chords give the air a jazzy feel, a bluesy feel, or even some new-age flavor. The second version of the tune contains many more embellishments than I would normally use, but it should give you some ideas for your own arrangement. I've applied the same concepts to the old-time fiddle tune "June Apple" on page 58.

The best rule to follow when creating your version is not to overdo it. One or two well-placed embellishments can add just the right touch to a piece and make the arrangement entirely your own.

Star of the County Down

Traditional, arranged by Dylan Schorer

MOVING ON

Track 62 Embellished Chords

June Apple

Traditional, arranged by Dylan Schorer

MOVING ON

Basic Chord Library

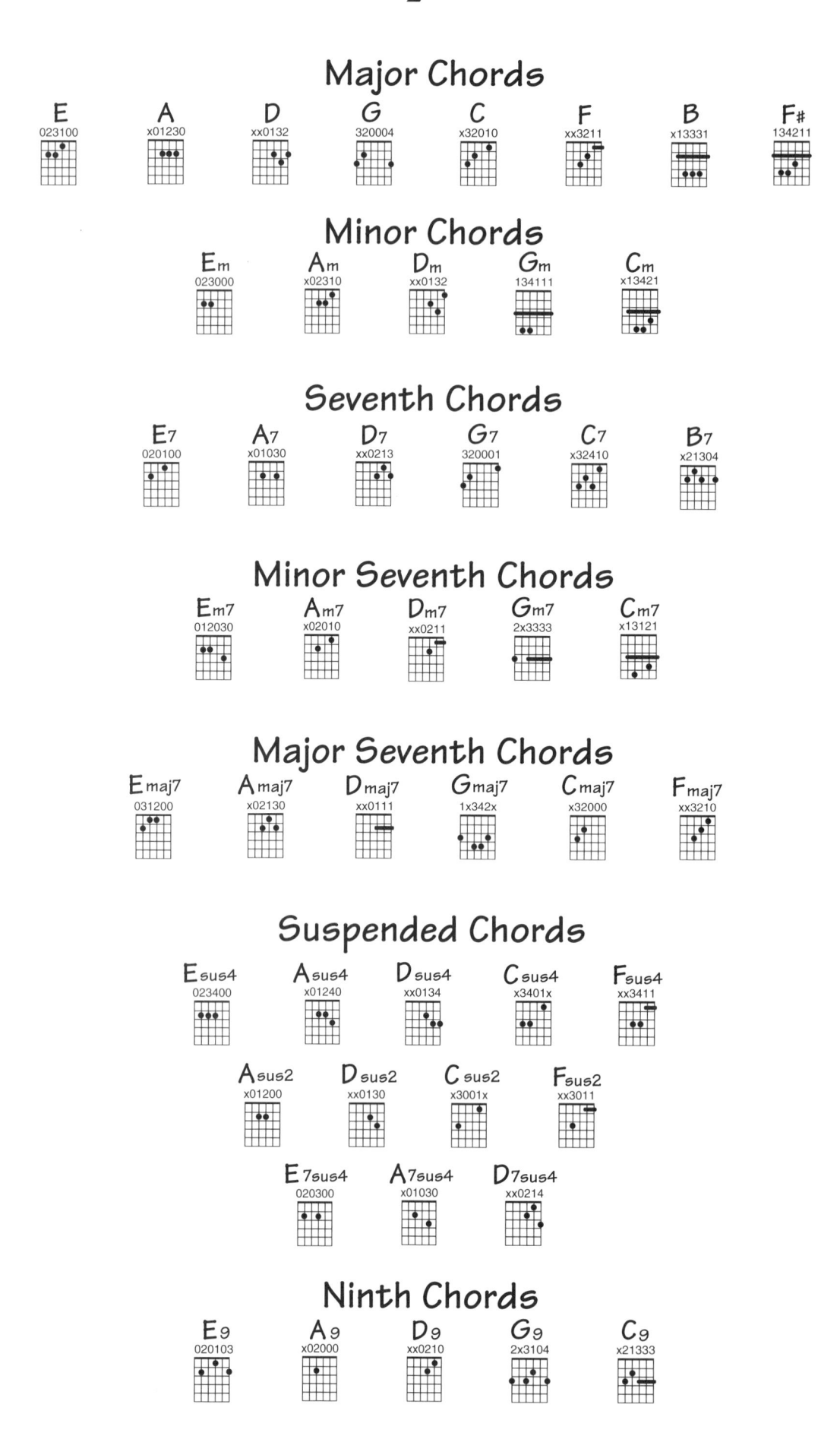

Major Chords

E	A	D	G	C	F	B	F#
023100	x01230	xx0132	320004	x32010	xx3211	x13331	134211

Minor Chords

Em	Am	Dm	Gm	Cm
023000	x02310	xx0132	134111	x13421

Seventh Chords

E7	A7	D7	G7	C7	B7
020100	x01030	xx0213	320001	x32410	x21304

Minor Seventh Chords

Em7	Am7	Dm7	Gm7	Cm7
012030	x02010	xx0211	2x3333	x13121

Major Seventh Chords

Emaj7	Amaj7	Dmaj7	Gmaj7	Cmaj7	Fmaj7
031200	x02130	xx0111	1x342x	x32000	xx3210

Suspended Chords

Esus4	Asus4	Dsus4	Csus4	Fsus4
023400	x01240	xx0134	x3401x	xx3411

Asus2	Dsus2	Csus2	Fsus2
x01200	xx0130	x3001x	xx3011

E7sus4	A7sus4	D7sus4
020300	x01030	xx0214

Ninth Chords

E9	A9	D9	G9	C9
020103	x02000	xx0210	2x3104	x21333

Subscribe today
(800) 827-6837

Or, place your order on our Web site!

www.acousticguitar.com

On every page of *Acoustic Guitar* Magazine, you'll recognize that same love and devotion you feel for your guitar.

Our goal is to share great guitar music with you, introduce you to the finest guitarists, songwriters, and luthiers of our time, and help you be a smarter owner and buyer of guitars and gear.

You'll also be getting the latest in gear news, artist interviews, practical player advice, songwriting tips, sheet music to play, music reviews, and more, every month.

Acoustic Guitar Magazine wants you to be happy. Let us show you how with a FREE issue. So subscribe now without any risk at the low introductory rate of $19.95 for 12 monthly issues, and enjoy a free issue compliments of *Acoustic Guitar* Magazine. You have our unconditional guarantee: You must be completely satisfied, or your payment will be refunded in full.

The best transcriptions of the best acoustic music

ACOUSTIC GUITAR Song

The editors of *Acoustic Guitar* are always listening to acoustic music. They publish the best songs and compositions they find in the pages of *Acoustic Guitar* magazine.

Now we're taking those same great songs and collecting them in the Acoustic Guitar Artist Songbooks. Folk, blues, bluegrass, rock, classical, swing, and more—you'll find it all in each eclectic collection.

With each songbook you get standard notation, guitar tablature, chord diagrams, artist bios, performance notes, and tips from the artists, all of which makes it easy to find and learn the song you want to play—there's no more searching for and leafing through back issues.

The bonus CD really brings the music to life. Now you

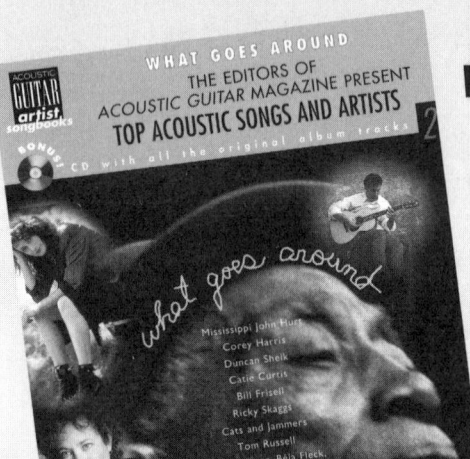

What Goes Around
Includes the full-length audio CD *What Goes Around*.

$16.95
Item #21699180

Habits of the Heart
Includes the full-length audio CD *Habits of the Heart*.

$16.95
Item #21699182

Sangisangy Dama
Wolf at the Door Patty Larkin
Embaixador Paulo Bellinati
At Seventeen Janis Ian
And So It Goes... Steve Tilston
Adriry D'Gary
I Still Want To Catie Curtis
Barely Breathing Duncan Sheik
Travis Edgar Meyer with Mike Marshall and Béla Fleck
The Sky Above, the Mud Below Tom Russell
Lover Come Back to Me Cats and Jammers
High Fever Blues Corey Harris
Louis Collins Mississippi John Hurt
Brother Bill Frisell
Knockin' on Your Door Muleskinner
Amanda Jewell Ricky Skaggs

Elliott Smith **Sweet Adeline**
Chris Whitley **Scrapyard Lullaby**
David Grier **Have You Ever Been to England**
Guy Davis **If You Love Somebody**
Mike Dowling **Rosalie**
Stephen Fearing **Coryanna**
Laura Love **I'm a Givin' Way**
Josh White **Landlord**
Jerry Douglas **A Tribute to Peador O'Donnell**
Merle Travis **Guitar Rag**
Roy Rogers **Gertie Ruth**
Dan Bern **Oh Sister**
Kristin Hersh **Home**
Scott Tennant **Mysterious Habitats**
Jim Croce **I'll Have to Say I Love You in a Song**

At your local music store or call Music Dispatch and order today!
(800) 637-2852

Distributed exclusively by
HAL•LEONARD